ISLAM AND NON-VIOLENCE

ISLAM AND NON-VIOLENCE

Dr. Mehboob Desai

GYAN

Islam and Non-violence

Rs. 625

ISBN: 978-81-212-1026-3

Published in 2009 in India by
Gyan Publishing House,
23 Main, Ansari Road, Darya Ganj,
New Delhi-110002
Phones : 23282060, 23261060
Fax : 011-23285914
E-mail: books@gyanbooks.com
Website: www.gyanbooks.com

Lasser Type Setting by: Quick Media, Delhi
Printed at : Singhal Print Media, Delhi

Dedicated

to

my

Father

Janab Usmanbhai Haji Husenbhai Desai

(2 July 1921 to 12 September 1998)

Still

my

Friend, Philosopher and Guide

Contents

PART - 3

Foreword

In the last two to three decades, humanity has witnessed considerable increase in violence. As Gandhi had predicted in Hind Swaraj, people do not hesitate carrying pistols with many chambers and do not hesitate opening fire at the slightest provocation. The group wars have been provided with more potent weapons of destruction. 'Formerly when people wanted to fight with one another, they measured between them bodily strength: now it is possible to take away thousands of lives by one man working behind a gun from a hill.' Gandhi wrote this in 1909 in Hind Swaraj. Things have changed further and now vast human destruction is possible by one man sitting at his home in cosy comfort and just pressing a button that will release a missile and hit the target hundreds of kilometres away. Unfortunately, the violence is not limited only to wars between nations or geo-political units, but different groups within a country or state express dissent violently.

A substantial number of groups that uses violence to express their dissent follow Islam religion. Some of these groups have been attempting rare acts of dare devilry and have been attacking civilian targets all over the world. These groups are equipped with latest weaponry. A characteristic feature of most of these groups, which now operate all over the world, is that they claim to be staunch followers of Islam. They are also blessed and supported by some Muslim religious masters. They consider themselves to be the soldiers of God out to defend the religion and the humanity. Clearly these are reactionary forces. The violent acts committed by these dissent groups have received immense publicity all over the world. They have come to be known as religious fundamentalists terrorising civilians.

It is not surprising that terrorisms have been linked with Muslim fundamentalism. This impression has received more exposure and acceptance in India and it has led to rise of Hindu fundamentalism in reaction. Obviously, this does not augur well for the people living in Indian sub continent and in other parts of the world.

We need to remember one of the great poets of the Indian sub continent Dr. Mohammad Iqbal here. *Majhab nahi sikhaata aapas me Bair rakhna*. Religion does not teach mutual hatred. Religion in its original form does not teach hatred and violence. This is also true for Islam. The book 'Islam and Non-Violence' by Dr. Mehboob Desai is topical and timely. It is not that the humanity did not know that Islam does not preach violence. It is just that there is a need to reaffirm this fact. Dr. Desai has attempted this in a modest way, but the message is conveyed. He has just gone to the basics. He tells readers that the basic principles of Islam do not suggest any violence. A good Muslim is one who believes and follows five fundamentals of *Shahada* (Creed), *Salat* (prayer), *Saum* (fasting), *Zakat* (paying annual Tax), *and Hajj* (Pilgrimage to Makkah). In following this there is no violence nor is there any scope for it. A rumour cannot be a historical fact or a theosophical truth says Dr. Desai. There is no truth in the statement that 'Islam has spread by sword'. In fact he narrates the whole sequence of the Great War that was fought by the Mohammad Paygamber and his small army. The Paygamber was attacked and he sought guidance from the God and then instructed his supporters only to defend and not to attack.

Dr. Desai has recounted the basic sayings in the Holy Quran and says in Chapter 3 of Part I, "All of them advise a Muslim to follow the right path, in right way, as gentle as possible, as righteous as possible." In this there is no advice and scope for violence. The book helps the readers to understand that the life of Mohammad Paygamber was based on peace and non-violence. The Paygamber was self-restrained and he showed mercy upon all. One can draw a lot of parallel between the Paygamber and Gandhi. Both loved the humanity immensely and approached people with compassion and understanding. Both believed and preached that humanity can survive well only if lived frugally and without being greedy and acquisitive. Paygamber who brought the message of God through the Quran clearly preached and followed the path of non violence. It is important to note that nowhere in Quran or in the life of the Paygamber violence for its own sake has been ever justified. ***Jehad*** has been another word which has been greatly misused, misinterpreted and abused by some of the followers of Islam and others who want to generate misinformation among non-Muslim people. The book has once again and in simple way brought out the true meaning of ***Jehad***. The author has tried to show that it is a concept similar to the one that has been preached in ***Geeta***. It is the fight between the good and the bad inside us. Gandhi also has written about Geeta with similar understanding. The fight of good and the bad is within.

The word terror is not to be found in whole of Quran and in the preaching of the Paygamber. The author has devoted a chapter to explain to readers that the word *Islam* means ease and peace. The greeting *Assalaam alaicum* means 'may peace be upon you'. These basic things should be ample for people to understand that violence has no place in Islam. The author has taken pains to tell the readers what Gandhi has selected from Quran to understand and show that Islam also was a religion that essentially preached peace, non violence and harmony with other fellow human beings and the nature.

Dr. Desai has planned this book more at a general plane than developing a scholarly thesis of Islam and non-violence. The book is in three parts. In Part I the author has provided basic tenets of Islam and tried to show how the religion came into being. It is clear in this part of the book that the basic religious text and other preaching by the Paygamber do not contain anything that justified violence in life and in practicing religion. In the second part, the author has used his training as a historian to recount in brief the life of Paygamber, his successful efforts to found the new religion, and the lives and times of Khalifas who carried the tradition forward. In this part Dr. Desai shows clearly that the Paygamber and his followers all preached and practiced a religion that was based on love and compassion and there was no scope for any kind of violence. Part III of the book contains stories from the lives of Paygamber and other famous Muslim saints. The anecdotes have been given in sufficiently large numbers to inform the readers that not only there is no violence in the basic tenets of Islam, but also the religious leaders who spread the message of Islam in the world followed lives that were based on non-violence and simplicity.

The common belief that Islam preaches violence and justifies for defending and spreading religion is a myth. Dr. Desai has made a good attempt to dispel it. I wish and hope that this book will receive wide attention and help in developing true understanding of Islam among both the believers and the non-believers.

Ahmedabad
April 2009

Sudarshan Iyengar
Vice Chancellor
Gujarat Vidyapeeth

Introduction

The majority of people may presume that there is no bond between Islam and non-violence. But, the non-violence is one of the fundamental principles of Islam. The people may wonder at the novelty of this presentation. Yet those who understand the real meaning of Islam, who have the concept of its philosophy, will not reject the claim of non-violence in Islam.

The first Surah of Holy Quran is named as 'Al Fatihah'. 'Al Fatihah' means 'to start or to begin'. Mohammad, the Messenger of Allah, peace be upon him, had called it as 'Ummul Quran'. 'Ummul Quran' means Mother of Quran. This Surah is festooned with words like mercy, praise, prayer, right way, etc. In this Surah it is prayed,

"In the name of Allah Most Gracious Most Merciful. Praise be to Allah the Cherisher and Sustainer of the Worlds. Most Gracious Most Merciful. Master of the Day of Judgment. Thee do we worship and Thine aid we seek. Show us the straight way. The way of those on whom Thou hast bestowed Thy Grace Those whose portion is not wrath and who go not astray.[1]

The first Surah of Holy Quran, namely 'Al Fatihah' is dedicated to Allah, Most Gracious. It is a prayer for success in a good action. There is no scope for violence in it. It never reflects on the violence, either directly or indirectly.

There is one incident referred in the Holy Quran. There were two sons of Adam, namely Habil or Abel and Qabil or Cain. The elder son of Adam, Cain, threatened Abel, the younger son of Adam with death. Then, Abel, the younger and righteous son of Adam replied to the bullying brother Cain.

"If thou dost stretch thy hand against me to slay me it is not for me to stretch my hand against thee to slay thee: for I do fear Allah the Cherisher of the worlds. For me I intend to let thee draw on thyself my sin as well as thine for thou wilt be among the companions of the fire and that is the reward of those who do wrong."[2]

With this belief in Islamic non-violence, and for fear of Allah the Cherisher of the worlds, Abel was readied to be martyred. Abel had followed the instructions of Allah the Cherisher of the worlds. For, Allah says in the Holy Quran,

"On that account: We ordained for the Children of Israel that if anyone slew a person unless it be for murder or for spreading mischief in the land it would be as if he slew the whole people:"[3]

Mahatma Gandhi, our Father of Nation, had expressed his opinion on the Islamic non-violence as under, "I have come to an opinion that the doctrine of Holy Quran is basically recommending the non-violence. In the Holy Quran, it is said that non-violence is better than violence. The order of implementation of violence should be done to fulfil the duty. The violence is permitted only that much as is necessary."[4]

There is a pre-concept of non-violence and a prejudice against the Islam. Populace believe that Muslims are basically violent, because of three Islamic tenets, namely Qurbani[5], Jehad[6] and permission for eating the flesh.[7] These tenets are making the populace to believe that there is the violence in Islam. But, these three things are allowed under certain limitations and for some special purpose only. So, we shall try to understand the real and theological meanings of them, and their practice in real sense. Then only we shall be able to understand the concept of non-violence in Islam. Firstly, it is necessary to understand the concept of non-violence, as preached by Jain Dharma and as practiced by our beloved Gandhiji.

The fundamental doctrine of Jain Dharma is non-violence. Gandhiji had adopted the best tenets from every living religion for his practical life, as well as for the guidance of his people in his Ashram. From the Jain Dharma, he had adopted the tenet of non-violence. He had adopted the concept of 'congregational prayers' and 'equality for all' in religious functions from the teachings of Islam. Certainly, there is a difference between the non-violence preached by Great Trithanker Mahavir of Jain Dharma, and the non-violence practiced by our Great National Leader, Mahatma Gandhi. The non-violence of Mahavir is delicately intricate and divine, whereas the non-violence being adopted and practiced by Mahatma Gandhi is humane in nature. When compared to these two kinds of non-violence, the Islamic non-violence is innate, sensible and practical.

As per the teaching of Jain Dharma, the present creation and the creature in it are not real in true sense. For the salvation from the false world, one should have to liberate himself from the eighteen misconducts, namely Prana-Atipata or Micro-violence, Mrushavad or Falsehood, Adattadan or Stealing, Maithun or Intercourse, Parigraha or Material Collection, Krodh or Anger, Ahankar or Arrogance, Maya or False Impression, Lobha or Greediness, Raga or Passion, Dwesha or Hatred, Kalah or Quarrelling, Abhyakhyan or Allegation, Paishun or Blaming, Rati or Emotion, Paraparivad or Accusation on others and Mithyatva or Blind Faith. To get rid of these eighteen entanglements of misconducts, Jain Dharma has shown four way-outs for human beings. These four jewels like way-outs are Samyagdrusti or True outlook, Samyaggyan or True Intelligence, Samyagvani or True speech and Samyagcharitra or True Conduct. These principles of Jain Dharma reveal that performance of violence by oneself, or making anyone to do violence, or permitting anyone for violence or tolerating anyone's violence are equal sins. Even a thought of killing an ant is a sin. Mercy is the Dharma for human being. I believe that this type of micro-nonviolence of Jain Dharma is aiming to achieve and to establish valuable dedication and good mannerism in human society.

Gandhiji had used Truth and Non-violence as his armour. Experimenting with Truth is the main magic of his manly verve. His concept of non-violence is very humane. He had recommended people to participate in bloodshed wars for a just cause. He had preferred to inject a deadly poison into a jick bullock in Ashram rather than to let it survive with unbearable pain and sufferings. Overall, he had not made the concept of non-violence as synonym to cowardice. He has declared his ideas about non-violence as under:

"Nonviolence is a concept which is cosmic and thick in nature. We are but ignorant creatures, which are encircled by the Holi-fire of violence. 'Living thing lives upon a living thing' is not a fallacy. Man cannot live for a minute without causing violence to other living things. While eating, sitting or in all his actions, intentionally or unintentionally he is bound to commit some kind of violence against other living things. If he endures the idea of endeavoring at his level best to protect even a small living thing from his violent actions, this passion makes him the worshiper of non-violence. In his conduct, there will be an ever-expanding restrait and an ever-spreading compassion. Yet, no one can achieve freedom from encircling superficial violence."[8]

We, as ordinary human beings, may accept the humane concept of non-violence of Gandhiji as simple and easily practicable as the delicately intricate and divine concept of non-violence of Jain Dharma, which is professed by Mahavir, the Great Tirthanker. Yet, the fallacious feeling of simplicity and adoptability of humane concept of non-violence may turn into a strong challenging act in practice.

References

1. The translation and meaning of 'Quran' in Gujarati by Mr. Ibrahim, Surat, Page No. 2. The English translation is quoted from 'Holy Quran', translated by Mr. Abdullah Yousuf Ali or by M. Pickthall.

2. Islam Darshan by Ismail Nagari, Sardar Patel University. Vallabh Vidyanagar, Page No. 93. "Holy Quran" - 5.27 to 5.30.
3. Holy Quran - 5.32.
4. Harijan Bandhu, 14 July 1940, p. 142.
5. "That they may witness the benefits provided for them and celebrate the name of Allah through the Days appointed over the cattle which He has provided for them for sacrifice : then eat ye thereof and feed the distressed ones in want. Holy Quran - 22.28.
6. Those who believe and suffer exile and strive with might and main in Allah's cause with their goods and their persons have the highest rank in the sight of Allah: They are the people who will achieve (salvation). Holy Quran - 9.20
7. Of the cattle are some for burden and some for meat. Eat what Allah hath provided for you and follow not the footsteps of Satan: for he is to you an avowed enemy—Holy Quran - 6.142.
8. Experiments with Truth - by M.K. Gandhi - Nav Jivan Prakashan - Ahmedabad, p. 304.

PART-1

1

Fundamentals of Islam

Gandhiji has explained the meaning of Islam by saying,

"The meaning of Islam is Peace. It is not related to Muslims only, but to all communities and to Universal Peace."[1]

Now, Islam is spread in every nook and corner of human world. The followers of Islam are called Muslims.[2] They are supposed to live non-violently. Islam is very necessary for the maintenance of peace in the world, now and in the future. It is true that the peace prevails due to non-violence. For the practice of non-violence in daily life, one must know the fundamentals of Islam. They are five in numbers. The speciality of these fundamentals is none of them preaches violence. Moreover, all of them recommend the Muslims for following the non-violence in thinking, in preaching and in practicing the daily livelihood actions. These five fundamentals of Islam are necessary for inculcating the non-violence in practical life.

The five fundamentals of Islam are Shahada or Creed[3], Salat[4] or Prayer, Saum[5] or Fasting, Zakat[6] or Purifying Annual Tax and Hajj[7] or Pilgrimage to Makkah as observed by Prophet Abraham, peace be upon him.

Shahada or Creed means belief in oneness of God. This concept is known as Tauhid in Islamic thought. Tauhid means to believe in that, 'God is One.' Hence, the alleged divine power shared by any other deemed Divinity, either physical or theosophical is completely rejected. So, it is said in Islam, "La Ilaha Illallah." As far as Mohammad, the Messenger of Allah, is concerned, all Muslims believe in that "Mohammad is the Messenger of God." So, it is declared, "Mohammadur Rasoolullah." Then, Mohammad, was chosen by God only to deliver the Word and Warning of Allah, the Cherisher of the worlds. The Shahada or Tauhid has been clarified as 'to believe only in Oneness of God.' As the Mohammad, the Messenger of Allah, would not be held responsible for the wrong doings of any human being, so, he had no compulsion to take the course of sword to compel any Arab or non-Arab to accept the Islam.

Salat[8] or Namaaz is a form of prayer. No doubt, a Prayer is dedicated to God, but it purifies the thoughts and body of a Muslim. The Book of God, Holy Quran ordains a Muslim to pray five times daily in normal conditions. When a Muslim child comes to certain age of understanding, then the prayer becomes obligatory on that child. The physical actions during the prayer are adopted from the Traditions of Mohammad, the Messenger of Allah. In fact, the procedure of prayer is very simple and pliable even for a child. The Traditions show us so many ways as to adjust ourselves in prayer according to our present conditions, positions and dress codes. Hence, there would be no violence of any kind in performing the physical actions of prayer or in reciting the sentences in prayer.

Now we come to the topic of Saum, Roza or Fasting. In every Creed of the current world, some kind of Fasting is religiously practiced. Many think the Fasting gives health for the physical body, as well as some purity for one's mental form. Islam does not intend to keep a Muslim fasting only for tolerating the pangs of hunger, thirst and of desires. Islam is intending to teach a Muslim to keep himself in Self-Restraint. During the Fasting, a Muslim is ordained to follow the three saintly monkeys that are "Never See Bad Thing," "Never Hear Bad Thing" and "Never Tell Bad

Thing." In addition, they have to follow the fourth monkey that "Never Do a Bad Thing." Almost, in a way, the four jewels of Jain Dharma, namely Samyagdrusti, Samyaggyan, Samyagvani and Samyagcharitra are followed by a Muslim during the period of Fasting. Our Lord ordains the Muslims to maintain the Fasting during the month of Ramadan. He says in Holy Quran,

"O Ye who believe! Fasting is prescribed to you as it was prescribed to those before you that ye may learn self-restraint. Fasting for a fixed number of days; but if any of you is ill or on a journey the prescribed number should be made up from days later. For those who can do it with hardship is a ransom the feeding of one that is indigent. But he that will give more of his own free will it is better for him and it is better for you that ye fast if ye only knew. Ramadan is the month in which was sent down the Quran as a guide to mankind also as clear Signs for guidance and judgment between right and wrong. So every one of you who is present at his home during that month should spend it in fasting but if anyone is ill or on a journey the prescribed period should be made up by days later. Allah intends every facility for you. He does not want to put you to difficulties. Allah wants you to complete the prescribed period and to glorify Him in that He has guided you; and perchance ye shall be grateful."[9]

During the Fasting, one should learn to keep himself in self-restraint, should learn to feed the hungry of one's own free will, to clarify the difference between the right doings and wrong doings, to be grateful of his Lord and to perform his duties at any time of the year. In either case, the intending pilgrim commences by putting on a simple garment of unsewn cloth in two pieces when a Muslim is at some distance yet from Makkah. The putting on of the pilgrim garb, called ihram, is symbolic of his renouncing the vanities of the world. When we closely observe a Muslim in ihram, at first sight, he seems to be a Jain Muni. His dress resembles to the dress of Jain Muni. A Muslim temporarily renounces the vanities of the physical world. Until the end of the pilgrimage, a Muslim must not wear other clothes, or ornaments, anoint his hair, use perfumes, hunt, or do other prohibited acts. The completion of the pilgrimage is symbolised by the shaving of the head for men, and the cutting off a few locks of the hair of the head for women, the putting off the ihram and the resumption of the ordinary dress.

Many Islamic scholars are of opinion that the Hajj is obligatory on one and all. But, as far as we know, the poor and the needy people, who cannot afford the expenses of Hajj, are freed from this duty. If a rich person is unable to perform a Hajj due to some unavoidable thing, he may assign someone else to perform Hajj on his behalf and at his expense. If one is afraid of one's life or of one's wealth due to something on way, then he is deemed to be as one who cannot afford the journey for Hajj. The person intending to perform Hajj should not sell his clothes, his personal belongings, or his house - even if they were abundant to get money for Hajj. Means of traveling imply that which enables him to go to Hajj and come back, whether it is by land, by sea, or by air.

The great financial burden and the good requirement of physical stamina may have caused some kind of violence on the intendant pilgrim. Allah is not intending to cause unnecessary violence to His believers. So, as per the wish of Allah, our Mohammad, the Messenger of Allah, had said,

"O People, listen to me in earnest, worship Allah, say your five daily prayers, fast during the month of Ramadan, and give your wealth in Zakat. Perform Hajj if you can afford to. You know that every Muslim is the brother of another Muslim. You are all equal. Nobody has superiority over other except by piety and good action."[10]

This Sermon of Mohammad, the Messenger of Allah, gives mental peace to the poor, unhealthy and helpless people, who had not performed the Hajj due to some reason. Due to this Sermon, a Muslim who had performed a Hajj cannot be proud of it, and a Muslim who had not performed ashamed of non-performance, because, nobody has superiority over other except duties as though they are not a burden on him. We have observed in the Sentences of Holy Quran that as Allah intends every facility for a Muslim, He does not want to put a Muslim to difficulty, no Muslim is expected to cause difficulty or violence to his body or mind. If one is not able to bear the pains of Fasting, he may feed another hungry man. Without learning the much-sought self-restraint and righteousness, if one goes on Fasting, he will suffer only the pangs of hunger, thirst and desires. If one observes the Saum in a right manner, the deemed violence of hunger, thirst and desire is eliminated.

The fourth fundamental of Islam is Zakat. We may say that Zakat is annual obligatory tax on the rich people. Many modern Economists feel that this Zakat is meant for the benefit of poor people. The Zakat may help the human society in taking out the extra amount from the rich people and to pass on the collected amount to the poor people. Even though the Zakat cannot eradicate the poverty from the society, in a way, a common cord connects the poor and rich people in the society, at least, in the month of Ramadan. Many Philosophers think that it is a way to provide 'Roti, Kapada Aur Makaan' to the poor. As some one is thinking, it may have been fixed at 2.5 per cent per annum on the rich people, to give that amount to the poor people, to eradicate the economic differences between them. The idea is logical. But, it is not factual. Zakat is not intended for that purpose only. As human beings, we know our wantonness for wealth. Every one of us is greedy of money, even if he is a billionaire. Yet, the Islam teaches a Muslim to spare something out of his wealth for the benefit of his poor brethren, if he is afraid of his Lord, the Cherisher of worlds. While calculating the amount of Zakat, one's own consciousness guides him to right estimation, more than 2.5%, without any guidance from any other Auditor or Inspector. In a way, Zakat teaches a Muslim to donate to his poor brethren at his own will and might. As there is no outer compulsion of any human official, no one feels any kind of violence in paying the Zakat. Moreover, to some extent, the receiver of Zakat will be relieved from the pangs of economical violence. As the feeding one is caring for the needy one, the scope of thefts and cheatings is certainly minimized. When such vices are eliminated, the scope of violence is also eliminated. In my view, the basic aim of Islam, the religion of peace, is to generate good relationship in humanity, and fear of God, and thus, to eliminate the root causes of violence.

The final fundamental of Islam is Hajj. Hajj means the pilgrimage to Makkah. The Hajj is the complete pilgrimage, of which the chief rites are during the first ten days of the month of Zul-Hajj. The Umra is a less formal pilgrimage by piety and good action. Where there is piety and good action, there is no place for violence.

References

1. Harijan Bandhu, 25 September 1940, p. 231.
2. The name of this religion is Islam, the root of which is Silm and Salam, which means peace. Salam may also mean greeting one another with peace. One of the beautiful names of God is that He is the Peace. It means more than that: submission to the One God, and to live in peace with the Creator, within one's self, with other people and with the environment. Thus, Islam is a total system of living. A Muslim is supposed to live in peace and harmony with all these segments; hence, a Muslim is any person anywhere in the world whose obedience, allegiance, and loyalty are to God, the Lord of the Universe.
3. Creed (Shahada): The verbal commitment and pledge that there is only One God and that Muhammad is the

Messenger of God, is considered to be the Creed of Islam. It is the basis of Islam.

4. The five obligatory prayers that a Muslim must perform everyday.
5. Fasting (Saum) : Fasting is total abstinence from food, liquids and intimate intercourse (between married couples) from dawn to sunset during the entire month of Ramadan.
6. Purifying Tax (Zakat) : This is an annual payment of a certain percentage of a Muslim's property, which is distributed among the poor or other rightful beneficiaries. The obligatory tax that every Muslim must give. It is one of the five pillars of Islam. The Zakat is used to provide for the poor and destitute.
7. Pilgrimage (Hajj) : The performance of pilgrimage to Makkah is required once in a lifetime if means are available. Hajj is in part in memory of the trials and tribulations of Prophet Abraham, his wife Hagar and his eldest son Prophet Ishmael, peace be upon them. Hajj means effort. The Hajj is the pilgrimage to Mecca that is obligatory on every Muslim. It is one of the five pillars of Islam and takes place during the Islamic month of Zhul al-Hijjah. A Muslim must perform the Hajj at least once in his life. The exception to this is financial and reasons of health.
8. Moreover, Salat was prescribed in order to reform and purify their souls, as if to say, "This is the thing which will produce in you those high qualities of character which are essential for everyone who intends to struggle in the righteous way." Incidentally, we learn from Traditions that Miraj was the first occasion on which the five daily Prayers were prescribed to be offered at fixed times.
9. Holy Quran - 2nd Surah -183 to 185.
10. This Sermon was delivered by Mohammad, the Messenger of Allah, on the Ninth Day of Dhul Hijjah 10 A.H. in the Uranah Valley of mount Arafat. It is quoted in Sahih Al Bukhari.

2

Spread of Islam

Ignorance of Islam has led the people to believe in the rumour, 'by sword, Islam has spread.' But a rumour cannot be an historical fact or a theological truth. Till now, no religion has won the hearts of millions of people by violence. There is much scope for scholastic studies to find out this evergreen truth. The charms of religious books, the charisma of religious saints, the conduct of its believers, the coordination in the colleagues in society influences the masses, thus, a religion spreads in the masses. Major Arthur Glean Leonard writes,

"If one considers a book due to its results and influence on the life of its readers, then, Quran is one of the Best Classical Books in the world."[1]

Islam is well spread, well read and well practiced religion in the world. Mohammad, the Messenger of Allah, was the first person to spread the religion of Islam. He lived a simple, submissive, supplicating life, which is a model for all Muslims, then, now and forever. He had never used his human force or sharpness of his sword to spread the Islam, because, Allah says,

"Let there be no compulsion in religion. Truth stands out clear from error; whoever rejects evil and believes in Allah hath grasped the most trustworthy handhold that never breaks. And Allah heareth and knoweth all things."[2]

Mohammad, the Messenger of Allah, was instructed by Allah in strict words. Mohammad, the Messenger of Allah, strictly adhered to the guidance given by our Lord. Some of the instructions that were given to Messenger of Allah Mohammad to propagate Islam are as under :

* "When you ask the people to embrace Islam, you teach them carefully and smoothly. When you discuss with them, use good and sweet words. When they argue with you, hear them with patience. Tolerate their argument. When you are departing from them, do it with compassion and gentleness."
* "If your Lord is willing, people would have accepted your words. Then, will you use force to make them follow your words?"
* "O You Mohammad! Allah has given you the knowledge. Follow it. Believe in One. There are no gods except Allah. Discard the worshipers of gods."
* "If Allah had willed, they would have worshiped One. You are not being sent as a Supervisor on them."[3]

Allah has ordained all people to love their parents and to follow their instructions without taking any objections. Yet, the compulsion in religion by them towards their children is not tolerable. Allah says,

"We have enjoined on man kindness to parents: but if they, either of them, strive to force thee to join with Me in worship anything of which thou hast no knowledge, obey them not. Ye have all to return to Me and I will tell you the truth of all that ye did."[4]

Mohammad, the Messenger of Allah, him, had followed the instructions given to him by his Lord, day and night. While spreading the message of Allah, he had implemented the sayings of Holy Quran without any innovations or modifications.

During the times of Mohammad, the Messenger of Allah, majority of Arabs were unlettered. Many of them were barbarians. The tradition of gambling, drinking, prostitution was very common. The traditional pride was making them bury their female children alive. The poor and the slaves were treated as animals. Tricking and cheating was common in business. Humanity and morality were lacking in the society. In such society, to start Islam from foundation, to raise it to zenith, we can imagine how hot and thorny it would have seem to Mohammad, the Messenger of Allah. It was difficult to teach anything to Arabs, for they were full of ignorance. Holy Quran discloses,

"The Arabs of the desert are the worst in unbelief and hypocrisy and most fitted to be in ignorance of the command which Allah hath sent down to his apostle: but Allah is All-Knowing All-Wise."[5]

Yet, Mohammad, the Messenger of Allah, had performed his duties with passion, compassion and patience. Pundit Sunderlal writes,

"Wherever Mohammad, the Messenger of Allah did go, the people used to make fun of him. They would make satirical remarks on his sayings. Whenever he would try to preach them the truth, they used to throw the dead animals' intestinal and fecal matter on him. His opponents warned the audiences, "Son of Abdulla is mad. Don't listen to him." Then, they would disturb his discourse by making disruptive noises, so that no one could hear him clearly. Many a time, he was stoned and was proned to bleeding."[6]

Under such strenuous conditions, Mohammad, the Messenger of Allah, had spent the first three years of his Prophethood at Makkah. During this time, he was able to make forty persons believe in his claims of Prophethood. Firstly, Lady Khadija, may Allah be pleased with her, readily accepted the creed of Islam. She was the eldest wife of Mohammad, the Messenger of Allah. The people, who had accepted the Islam at initial stage, were Ali, who was ten-year-old son of Abu Talib, Zaid, Abu Bakr, Osman, and others who were well guided by Allah. Most of them were poor people. Many of them were slaves.

Even though Mohammad, the Messenger of Allah, had faced many hurdles, physical pressures, pains, stresses and strains of brain in his struggle to propagate Islam, he had never deserted the straight path of Islam due to disappointments or displeasures. Mohammad, the Messenger of Allah, had followed the instructions of Allah with patience and non-violence. His approach towards the populace with endurance and nonviolent attitude had owned the hearts of majority of Arabs, the patient and non-violent attitude had mesmerised the pagan Arabs, who were accustomed to pride, prejudice and brutality.

Not only in Hindustan but also in other countries, Islam has spread. The part played by Islamic saints in the propagation of Islam is praiseworthy. The conditions of human society have also given a momentum to this propagation of Islam. Everywhere, the society is divided between rich and poor, powerful and powerless, stupid and prudent. The rulers are arrogant and autocratic. Either the justice is utterly denied or unduly delayed for the meek. But, during the times of Mohammad, the Messenger of Allah, rich and poor were treated as equal. In the eyes of a Muslim, both an Amir and his slave were equal. Justice was done to all. Then, the four righteous Caliphs, namely, Abu-Bakr, Omar, Osman and Ali, may Allah be pleased with them, had followed the same traditions. Then, the preachers, saints and administrators of Islamic kingdoms have tried to follow the same traditions of endurance and non-violence.

Thereafter, the time of sultanate arrived. In Islam, no man would call himself a Malik or a King. Everyone is an Abdul-Malik or a slave of King. The Real King is Allah.

Islamic society represents a democratic setup, not an autocratic or patriarchic setup. The power of administration should be given to a person, who is most piteous, righteous, and best knower of Holy Quran. The power of administration never goes to an heir of administrator by birth. This rightful tradition was overpowered by other generations. The tradition of violence was encouraged. Wise ones were driven back. Warriors were given the thrones. They were entitled as King of Kings. Their word became the Word of God. Such kings had adopted the way of violence in propagating their faith. This thing did happen in all countries, irrespective of Islamic and non-Islamic cultures. Some scholars refer to the fanaticism of Aurangzeb, the King of Hindustan. Neither his fanaticism nor anybody's fanaticism is taught by Holy Quran or by the Traditions of Mohammad, the Messenger of Allah. By using his powers, no king could make his people believe in his own religion whole-heartedly. So, not only Islam, but also no other religion could have been propagated through the generations with the mighty power of sword. Hence, there is no place for violence in Islamic propagation.

Islam teaches discriminate non-violence. No compulsion or coercion is allowed in the propagation of Islam. A preacher should have to tell about the facts of Islam, 'the Oneness of God' clearly, diligently without malice towards anybody. A preacher will not be held responsible for the acts of either believer or non-believers, who go astray. A preacher will be awarded for teaching what is taught by Holy Quran. Allah says,

"Thus do We explain the Signs by various symbols: that they may say, "Thou hast taught us diligently" and that We may make the matter clear to those who know. Follow what thou art taught by inspiration from thy Lord: there is no god but He : and turn aside from those who join gods with Allah. If it had been Allah's Plan, they would not have taken false gods: but We made thee not one to watch over their doings, nor art thou set over them to dispose of their affairs.

Revile not ye those whom they call upon besides Allah lest they out of spite revile Allah in their ignorance. Thus have We made alluring to each people its own doings. In the end will they return to their Lord and We shall then tell them the truth of all that they did."[7]

References

1. Major Arthur Glean Leonard, Islam - Page No. 105-106.
2. Holy Quran - 2-256-" La_ikra_ha fid din(i), qad tabayyanar rusydu minal gaiy (i), famay yakfur bit ta_gu_ti wa yu'mim billa_hi fa qadistamsaka bill 'urwatil wusqa_lanfisa_ma laha_, walla_hu sami'un 'alim(un)".
3. "Geeta Ane Quran" by Pundit Sunderlal, Nav Jivan Prakashan, Ahmedabad. Page No. 178-179.
4. Holy Quran - 29. 8
5. Holy Quran - 9-97 – "Al a'ra_bu aside kufraw wa nifa_qaw wa ajar alla_ ya'lamu_ hudu_da ma_anzalalla_ hu'ala_rasu_jih (i), walla_hu'alimun hakim (un)."
6. "Hazarat Mohammad Ane Islam" by Pundit Sunderlal, Nav Jivan Prakashan, Ahmedabad. Page No. 37-38.
7. Holy Quran-6-105-109. "Wa kaza_ljika nusarriful a_ya_ti wa liyaqu_lu_ arista wa linubayyinahu_liqaumiy ya'lamu_n (a). Italic' ma_ u_hiya iliac mir rabbi (a), la_ ila_ha ill_ huw (a), wa a'rid 'anil musyrikin (a). Wa lau sya_'alla_hu ma_ asyraku_, wa ma_ ja'alna_ka'alaihim hafiz_ (n), wa ma_ anta 'alaihim bi wakil (in). Wa la_ tasubbul lazina yad'u_na min du_nilla_hifa yasubbulla_ha 'adwam bi gairi 'ilm (in), kaza_lika zayyanna_ likulli ummatin'amalahum, summa ila_ rabbihim marji'uhum fa yunabbi'uhum bima_ ka_nu_ ya'malu_n(a)."

3

Non-violence in Holy Quran

Before we discuss non-violence in Holy Quran, it is necessary to know about Holy Quran. We all know that the religious book of Muslims is Holy Quran. It is revealed in Arabic. But, it is not written by Mohammad, the Messenger of Allah, who was unlettered, but wise, trustworthy and righteous Arab. Even Allah had not declared the Holy Quran at one glance, as Shri Krishna had done about Bhagavad-Gita. The Lord of Universe has intended to guide the common populace to the right path, through the teachings of Holy Quran. He has set a Beautiful Model in the life of Messenger of Allah. Since the day of appointing Mohammad bin Abdulla as Prophet of Allah, the Sentences of Holy Quran had been taught to Mohammad, the Messenger of Allah, through the medium of Jibrail, in stages. Allah says in Holy Quran,

"It is We Who have sent down the Qur'an to thee by stages."[1]

Mohammad, the Messenger of Allah, was taught ways to live a righteous life of a Muslim, and he was warned to avoid certain things to achieve his aim. This Holy Quran had reached Mohammad, the Messenger of Allah, in parts, which we know as 'Wahi' or 'Revelation'. It took 23 years to reveal the whole of Holy Quran. The Holy Quran consists of 114 Surahs. As our Lord has promised, the Holy Quran is the exact word of Allah; its authenticity, originality and totality are intact. The Qur'an is the exact word of God; its legitimacy, creativity and entirety are intact.

Every aspect of human life, like love and worship, kindheartedness and forgiveness, diplomacy and dealings with others, regularity and legitimacy, parity and amity, relationship with others and tolerance of others is taught to Mohammad, the Messenger of Allah, in this Holy Quran.

The Islamic history tells us that the first Sentence of Holy Quran that was revealed to Mohammad, the Messenger of Allah, in the month of Ramadan. The first Sentence is in the Surah Al-Alaq. It is the 96th Surah in the Holy Quran. The summary of Islam is told at a time in a single Surah Al-Alaq. It deals with the importance of knowledge of reading to a Muslim. A Muslim must know how to read and write and what to read and write. A Muslim must know the facts of his generation, he must know how to use the pen. He should know what is yet not known to him. While acquiring knowledge, he must not transgress natural legitimacy. He should not pride himself. One day, a man shall have to return to his Lord. He will be held responsible for his deeds. So, he should worship One God. Let a Muslim be not adhered to Satanic advices. Let him be a sincere, closer subordinate to Allah. — Thus, Surah Al-Alaq ordains,

"Read! In the name of thy Lord and Cherisher Who created, Created man out of a mere clot of congealed blood: Read! And thy Lord is Most Bountiful. He Who taught the use of the Pen. Taught man that which he knew not. Nay but man doth transgress all bounds. In that, he looketh upon himself as self-sufficient. Verily to thy Lord is the return of all. Seest thou one who forbids. A votary when he turns to pray? Seest thou if He is on the road of Guidance? Or enjoins Righteousness? Seest thou if he denies Truth and turns away? Knoweth he not that Allah doth see? Let him beware! If he desist not, We will drag him by the forelock, A lying sinful forelock! Then let him call for help to his council of comrades: We will call on the angels of punishment to deal with him! Nay heed him not: but bow down in adoration and bring thyself the closer to Allah!"[2]

When we see the hand-written or printed Holy Quran, the first Sentence we see is "Bismilla_hir rahma_nir rahim (i)", which means "In the name of Allah Most Gracious Most Merciful." That is, Allah is charitable to all, even though they are not worthy of it. Allah is generous to those people, who maintain the relationship in righteousness. In both of these cases, He shows love, kindness, and non-violence towards the mankind. There are so many Sentences, which deal with love, kindness and non-violence. Such as,

- "Say: "If ye do love Allah follow me: Allah will love you and forgive you your sins for Allah is Oft-Forgiving Most Merciful."[3]
- "How many are the creatures that carry not their own sustenance? It is Allah Who feeds both-them and you: for He hears and knows all things."[4]
- "There is not a single one on earth which is not provided by Lord. He knows its existence and its abode at the end."
- "Allah has bestowed His gifts of sustenance more freely on some of you than on others; those more favored are not going to throw back their gifts to those whom their right hands possess so as to be equal in that respect. Will they then deny the favors of Allah?"[5]
- "And in no wise covet those things in which Allah hath bestowed his gifts more freely on some of you than on others: to men is allotted what they earn and to women what they earn: but ask Allah of His bounty: for Allah hath full knowledge of all things."[6]

- "And obey Allah and His apostle; and fall into no disputes lest ye lose heart and your power depart; and be patient and persevering: for Allah is with those who patiently persevere."[7]
- On that Day will men proceed in companies sorted out to be shown the Deeds that they had done. Then shall anyone who has done an atom's weight of good see it![8]
- "Nor could they spend anything (for the cause) small or great, nor cut across a valley, but the deed is inscribed to their credit; that Allah might requite their deed with the best (possible reward)."[9]
- "Never did We destroy a population but had its warners. By way of reminder; and We never are unjust."[10]
- "And the Book of Deeds will be placed before you; and thou wilt see the sinful in great terror because of what is recorded therein; they will say "Ah! Woe to us! what a book is this! It leaves out nothing small or great but takes account thereof!" They will find all that they did place before them: and not one will thy Lord treat with injustice."[11]
- "He is the One that accepts repentance from His Servants and forgives sins: and He knows all that ye do. And He listens to those who believe and do deeds of righteousness and gives them expanse of His Bounty: but for the Unbelievers there is a terrible Penalty. If Allah were to enlarge the provision for His Servants they would indeed transgress beyond all bounds through the earth; but He sends it down in due measure as He pleases: for He is with His Servants well-acquainted Watchful".[12]
- "Why should your Lord give you all sufferings unnecessarily, if you are showing gratitude towards Allah, and study fast on right path."

- "And if ye do catch them out, catch them out no worse than they catch you out: but if ye show patience that is indeed the best course for those who are patient."[13]
- "O ye who believe! seek help with patient perseverance and prayer: for Allah is with those who patiently persevere."[14]
- They said: "Art thou indeed Joseph?" He said: "I am Joseph and this is my brother: Allah has indeed been gracious to us all: behold he that is righteous and patient, never will Allah suffer the reward to be lost of those who do right."[15]
- "And say: "Work righteousness: soon will Allah observe your work and His apostle and the believers: soon will ye be brought back to the knower of what is hidden and what is open: then will He show you the truth of all that ye did."[16]
- "Behold ye are those invited to spend of your substance in the way of Allah: but among you are some that are niggardly. But those who are niggardly are so at the expense of their own souls. But Allah is free of all wants and it is ye that are needy. If ye turn back from the Path, He will substitute in your stead another people; then they would not be like you!"[17]
- "When a courteous greeting is offered, you meet it with a greeting still more courteous at least of equal courtesy. Allah takes careful account of all things."[18]
- "But if the enemy inclines towards peace do thou also incline towards peace and trust in Allah: for He is the one that heareth and knoweth all things."[19]
- "They ask thee concerning wine and gambling. Say: "In them is great sin and some profit for men; but the sin is greater than the profit." They ask thee how

much they are to spend; say: "What is beyond your needs." Thus, doth Allah make clear to you His Signs: in order that ye may consider."[20]

- "O ye who believe! intoxicants and gambling, dedication of stones and divination by arrows are an abomination of Satan's handiwork: eschew such abomination that ye may prosper. Satan's plan is but to excite enmity and hatred between you with intoxicants and gambling and hinder you from the remembrance of Allah and from prayer: will ye not then abstain?"[21]
- "We know best what they say; and thou art not one to ever awe them by force. So admonish with the Qur'an such as fear My Warning!"[22]

I have given an iota out of bunches of good sayings, which are abundant in Holy Quran. All of them advise a Muslim to follow the right path, in right way, as gently as possible, as righteously, as possible. They are prohibiting the items and routes, which are root to create the vice and violence.

When Gandhiji read the Holy Quran, which is full of such serene sayings, he expressed his opinion,

"Mohammad is an Artist. His Quran is treated as best book out of the beautiful books of Arabic language. Even the pundits are also opining the same. What is the reason? The reason is, whatever facts he had observed, he had disclosed in it."[23]

References

1. Holy Quran - 76 -23. "In na_ nahnu naz zalna_ alaikal qur a_na tanzila" _
2. Holy Quran - 96-1-19 "Iqra bismi rabikal lazi halaq, Halakal insa_na min alaq, Iqra wa rabukal akram, Alazi alama bill qalam, Alamal insa_na ma_ lam yalam, Kala_ inal insa_na layatga. Ar ra a_hus tagna_, Ina ila_ rábika ruja_, Ara aita lazi yanha_, Abdan iza_ sala_. Ara aita in

ka_na alal huda_, Au amara bit taqwa_, Ara aita in kazaba wa tawa la_, Alam yalam bi anal la_ha yara_, Kala_ lail lam yantahi lanasfaam bin na_siyah. Na_siyatin ka_zibatin kha_tiah. Falyadu na_diyah, Sanaduz zaba_niyah. Kala_ la_ tutihu wasjud waqtarib."

3. Holy Quran-3-31- "Qul in kuntum tuhibbu_nalla_ha fattabi'u_ni yuhbibkumulla_hu wa yagfirlakum zunu_bakum, walla_hu gafu_rur rahim (un)."
4. Holy Quran-29-60-"Wa ka ay yim min da_b batil la_ tahmilu. rizqaha_ al la_hu yarzuquha_ wa iyya_kum wa huwas samiul alim".
5. Holy Quran-16-71-"Walla_hu faddala ba'dakum 'ala_ ba'din fir rizq (i), famal lazina fuddilu_ bira_ddi rizqihim 'ala_ ma_ malakat aima_nuhum fahum fihi sawa_'(un), fabini'matilla_hiyajhadu_n (a)."
6. Holy Quran-4-32- "Wa la_ tatamannau ma_ faddalalla_hu bihi ba'dakum'ala_ ba'd (in). Ur rija_linasibum mimmaktasabu_, wa linnisa_'i nasibum mimmaktasabn (a), was'alulla_ha min fadlih (i), innalla_ha ka_na bi kulli syai'in 'alima_ (n).
7. Holy Quran-8-46. – "Wa ati'ulla_ha wa rasu_lahu_ wa la_ tana_za'u_ fa tafsyalu_ wa tazhaba rihukum wasbiru_, innalla_ha ma'as sa_birin (a)."
8. Holy Quran-99- 6-7- Yauma idziy yashdurun na_su asyta_ tal Uyurau ama_lahum. Famay ya mal mitsqa_la dzar ratin khairay yarah.
9. Holy Quran-9-121- Wa la_ yunfiqu_na nafaqatan sagirataw wa la_ kabirataw wa la_yaqta'a_na wa_diyan ill_ kutiba lahum liyajziyahumulla_hu ahsana ma_ ka_nu_ ya'malu_n(a).
10. Holy Quran-41-208-209. "Wa ma_ ahlakna_ min qaryatin il la_ laha_ munziru_n. Zikra_ wama_ kun na_ za_limin."
11. Holy Quran-18-49- "Wa wudi'al kita_bu fataral mujrimina musyfiqina mimma_ fihi wa yaqu_lu_na ya_ wailatana_ ma_li ha_zal kita_bi la_ yuga_diru sagirataw wa la_ kabiratan ill_ ahsa_ha_, wa wajadu_ ma_ 'amilu_ ha_dira_(n), wa la_ yazlimu rabbuka".

12. Holy Quran-42-25-26-27- Wa huwal lazi yaqbalut taubata an iba_dihi wa yafu_ anis say yi a_ti wa yalamu ma_ tafalu_n. Wa yastajibul lazina a_manu_ wa amilus sa_liha_ti wa yaziduhum min fadlih wal ka_firu_na lahum aza_bun sadid. Walau basatal la_hur razqa liiba_dihi labagau fil ardi wa la_kiy yunaz zilu biqadarim ma_ yasya_ in nahu_ bi iba_dihi kabirun basir."
13. Holy Quran-16-126- "Wa in 'a_qabtum fa 'a_qibu_ bi misli ma_ 'u_qibtum bih (i), wa la'in sabartum lahuwa khairul us sa_birin (a)."
14. Holy Quran - 2 - 156- "Ya_ ayyuhal lazina a_manus ta'inu_ bis sabri was sala_h (ti), innalla_ha ma'as sa_birin (a)."
15. Holy Quran - 12-90- Qa_lu_ a'innaka la'anta yu_suf (u), qa_la ana yu_sufu wa ha_za_ akhi qad mannalla_hu 'alaina_, innahu_ may yattaqi wa yasbir fa innalla_ha la_ yudi'u ajral muhsinin (a).
16. Holy Quran - 9 - 105 – "Wa qul-i'malu_ fasayaralla_hu 'amalakum wa rasu_luhu_ wal mu'minu_n (a), wa saturaddu_na ila_ 'a_limil gaibi wasy syaha_dati fayunabbi'ukum bima_ kuntum ta'malu_n (a)."
17. Holy Quran-47-38- "Ha_ antum ha_ ula_i tadauna litunfiqu_ fi sabilil la_h fa minkum may yabkhalu wa may yabkhal fa in nama_ yabkhalu an nafsih wal la_hul ganiyu wa antumul fuqara_u wa in yastabdil qauman gairakum suma la_ yaku_nu_amsa_lakum".
18. Holy Quran - 4 - 86.- "Alla_hu la_ ila_ha ill_ huw(a), layajma'annakum ila_ yaumil qiya_matila_ raiba fih(i). wa man asdaqu minalla_hi hadisa_(n)."
19. Holy Quran - 8-61- "Wa in janahu_ lis salmi fajnah laha_ wa tawakkal 'alalla_h (i), innahu_ huwas sami'ul 'alim (u).
20. Holy Quran – 2 - 219. "Fid dunya_ wal a_khirah(ti), wa yas'alu_naka 'anil yata_ma_ qulisla_hul lahum khair(un), fa in tukhalitu_hum fa ikhwa_nukum, walla_hu ya'lamul mufsida minal muslih(i), wa lau sya_ 'alla_hu la'a'natakum innalla_ha 'azizun hakim(un)."
21. Holy Quran - 5-90-91. "Ya_ ayyuhal lazina a_manu_ innamal khamru wal maisiru wal ansa_bu wal azla_mu

rijsum min 'amalisy syaita_ni fajtanibu_hu la'allakum tuflihu_n (a). Innama_ yuridusy syaita_nu ay yu_qi'a bainakumul 'ada_wata wal bagda_'a fil khamri wal maisiri wa yasuddakum 'an zikrilla_hi wa 'anis sala_ti fahal antum muntahu_n (a)."

22. Holy Quran - 50-45. "Nahnu alamu bima_ yaqu_lu_na wa ma_ anta alaihim bijab ba_rin fazakir bill qur a_ni may yaka_fu wajid".

23. Nav Jivan- 2nd November 1924, p. 72.

4

Mohammad and Non-violence

Mohammad (the Messenger of Allah) and Non-violence

The life of Mohammad, the Messenger of Allah, (peace be upon him,) was based on the foundation of peace and non-violence. Since his childhood to his young age, he was called as 'trustworthy' and 'modest' even by the pagan Arabs. During the period of Prophethood, while propagating the Islam, he had faced many hurdles, insults, and difficulties; yet, he had not deserted his nature of composure, compassion and patience. The instructions of Holy Quran, such as 'No compulsion in religion' and "No fighting" were strictly followed. Mohammad, the Messenger of Allah, had spent whole of his life as patiently and piously as humanly possible without any arrogance and pride. It was inscribed on the sword of Mohammad, the Messenger of Allah,

"Forgive him who wrongs you; join him who cuts you off; do good to him who does evil to you; and speak the truth even if it be against yourself."[1]

As Abdulla Bin Amr has narrated, once a man asked the Messenger of Allah, "What sorts of deeds of Islam are good?" The Messenger of Allah replied, "To feed the poor, to greet whom you know and also to those whom you do not know."[2]

While explaining the relationship with neighbours, Mohammad, the Messenger of Allah said, "He is not a Muslim, who feeds himself while his neighbour is hungry." By following the tradition of Messenger of Allah, Umar Ibn al-Khattab said, "Does one of you want to fill his belly keeping apart from his neighbour or nephew? How can you overlook this Ayat? 'You squandered your good things in the life of this world and sought comfort in them.' (Sura 46 Ayat 20)."[3]

Holy Quran orders a Muslim to help his neighbour. It says,

"Serve Allah and join not any partners with Him: and do good to parents, kinsfolk, orphans, those in need-neighbors who are near neighbors, who are strangers, the companion by your side, the way-farer (ye meet) and what your right hands possess: for Allah loveth not the arrogant, the vainglorious."[4]

While explaining about the qualities of a Muslim, Messenger of Allah said,

"Don't nurse grudge and don't bid him out for raising the price and don't nurse aversion or enmity and don't enter into a transaction when the others have entered into that transaction and be as fellow-brothers and servants of Allah. A Muslim is the brother of a Muslim. He neither oppresses him nor humiliates him, nor looks down upon him. The piety is here, (and while saying so) he pointed towards his chest thrice. It is a serious evil for a Muslim that he should look down upon his brother Muslim. All things of a Muslim are inviolable for his brother in faith; his blood, his wealth and his honour."[5]

Messenger of Allah always loved to protect the lives of animals and birds. Once the Messenger of Allah and his companions were travelling. Abdullah Ibn Mas'ud narrated,

"One day we saw a bird with her two young offsprings. We captured the two young offsprings. The bird came and began to spread its wings. The Messenger of Allah, came and said: "Who grieved this for its young ones? Return its young ones to it." He also saw honey bee that we had burnt. He asked: "Who has burnt this?" We replied: "We." He said: "It is not proper to punish with fire except the Lord of fire."[6]

The above incident shows the non-violent nature of Mohammad, the Messenger of Allah. He prohibited even stealing of eggs from the nests of birds. Abu Huraira narrated it,

"The Messenger of Allah said, "Allah curses a man who steals an egg and gets his hand cut off, or steals a rope and gets his hands cut off."[7]

Mohammad, the Messenger of Allah, did not like to eat Onion and Garlic. But, he did not force his people not to eat the Garlic, Onion etc. Abu Ayub Ansari narrated,

"When food was brought to Messenger of Allah, he ate out of that, and sent the remaining part to me. One day, he sent to me the leftover; I found that he had not taken from it at all, for it included garlic. I asked him whether that was forbidden, whereupon he said: "No, but I do not like it because of its odour." Then I said: "Then I also do not like what you do not like."[8]

The reason for not eating the garlic and onions by Messenger of Allah, was revealed by himself. The garlic and onion were not prohibited by Allah. But any bad smell was not befitting to a good man, while he would be talking to holy persons. Jabir Bin Abdullah narrated,

"The Messenger of Allah said, "Whoever has eaten garlic or onion should keep away from us, or should keep away from our mosque and should stay at home." Ibn Wahb said, "Once a plate full of cooked vegetables was brought to the Messenger of Allah at Badr. Detecting a bad smell from it, he asked about the dish and he was informed of the kinds of vegetables it contained. He then said, "Bring it near," and so it was brought near to one of his companions who was with him. When the Messenger of Allah saw it, he disliked eating it and said to his companion, "Eat, for I talk in secret to ones whom you do not talk to."[9]

Abu Sayed Al Kudri narrated,

"We made no transgression but Khaybar was conquered. We, the Companions of the Messenger of Allah, fell upon this plant, *i.e.* garlic, because the people were hungry. We ate it to our heart's content and then made our way towards the mosque. The Messenger of Allah, sensed its odour and he said: He who takes anything of this offensive plant must not approach us in the mosque. The people said: "Its use has been forbidden; its use has been forbidden." This reached the Messenger of Allah. He said: "O people, I cannot forbid the use of a thing, which Allah has made lawful, but this garlic is a plant, the odour of which is repugnant to me."[10]

Even though Mohammad, the Messenger of Allah, was having a full control over his people, he never forced his will and wish on his followers. He told the truth. He lived a simple life. He dedicated his life to the worship of Allah. Yet, he never overlooked his responsibility towards his family and his people. He never wore Silk or any other costly cloth that was a show-off of rich people. He was not fond of rich food. He normally used a white cloth to cover his body. He talked with others simply and sincerely. He treated rich and poor alike. His behaviour was full of love and compassion. While he was alive, the Islam had spread. Yet, he had not shown his authority as normal kings would have done. He never sat on a throne. He never wore a crown. He never attired in a sacerdotal gown. He never lived in a mansion. He lived in a mud cottage, with a top of palm tree leaves. Every one was freely allowed to meet him, irrespective of his age, nationality, race and religion. He loved the children very much. He used to play with children in the streets. He used to visit the sickly people at their homes. He was accustomed to accompany a Muslim or a non-Muslim, while bidding him goodbye. He never rejected an invitation, even by a poor-man or by a slave. These special characteristics were naturally seen in his life.

In the book, 'Life of Mohammad', Sir W. Mure wrote,

"He conducted himself with love and respectful even with common people. When he did walk, he walked respectfully. He showed mercy upon all. If any body irritated him by a word or deed, he was not offended. He was self-restraint. He was lenient. He generously donated. These qualities had made him loved by all, who were around him."

References

1. Hazarat Mohammad Ane Islam by Pundit Sunderlal - Nav Jivan Prakashan – Ahmedabad, pp. 37-38.
2. Book 2- Belief - 1.11. Sahih Al Bukhari.
3. Al-Muwatta- 49.36.
4. Holy Quran-4.3B-Wa'budulla_ha wa la_ tusyriku_ bihi syai'aw wa bill wa_lidaini ihsa_naw wabizil qurba_ wal yata_ma_ wal masa_kini wal ja_rizil qurba_ wal ja_ril junubi was sa_hibi bill jambi wabnis sabil(i), wa ma_ malakat aima_nukum, innalla_ha la_ yuhibbu man 'ka_na mukhta_lan fakhu_ra_(n).
5. Sahih Muslim Hadith-6219.
6. Sunan Abu Dawood-Hadith-2669.
7. Sahih Al-Bukhari, Hadith-8-774.
8. Sahih Al-Bukhari-Hadith-5097.
9. Sahih al-Bukhari- Hadith- 9-458.
10. Sahih Al-Muslim-Hadith-1149.

5

Wars and Non-violence

Since his childhood, Mohammad, the Messenger of Allah, peace be upon him, was loved by all in Makkah. In his teen age and youth, he was praised as 'Trustworthy' and 'Modest'. But, as soon as he started propagating the teachings of Islam, for thirteen years, he faced the people of Makkah as hostile as they could be. He lived in negative atmosphere and tolerated all types of hurdles created by his neighbours and relatives, not to speak of other citizens. The people of Makkah took him and his followers to task. During these thirteen years, many Ayats of Holy Quran were revealed to him. These Ayats were full of advice to Mohammad, the Messenger of Allah, to keep patience and tolerance against the maltreatment and misbehaviour of people of Makkah and other pagan people. He was advised to live a righteous, pious and patient life even in those treacherous conditions.

Thereafter, Mohammad, the Messenger of Allah, migrated to Yathrib along with a few of his followers. This migration is called Hijrat. Then, many people reached there. Yathrib became Madinah, or a City. Mohammad, the Messenger of Allah was not spared in this city also. The people of Makkah had tried their level best to kill Mohammad, the Messenger of Allah, who was staying then in Madinah. The people of Makkah gathered an army to attack Madinah. Then, for the first time in Holy Quran, Mohammad, the Messenger of Allah, was guided to defend himself against those offensives by the pagan people. The permitting Ayat of Holy Quran reads.

"To those against whom war is made, permission is given to fight, because they are wronged. Verily, Allah is Most powerful for their aid. They are those, who have been expelled from their homes in defiance of right for no cause except that they say, "Our Lord is Allah." Had Allah not checked one set of people by means of another, there would surely have been pulled down monasteries, churches, synagogues and mosques in which the name of Allah is commemorated in abundant measure. Allah will certainly aid those who aid His cause; for verily Allah is Full of Strength Exalted in Might, Able to enforce His Will. (They are) those who, if We establish them in the land, establish regular prayer and give regular charity, enjoin the right and forbid wrong: with Allah rests the end (and decision) of (all) affairs."[1]

The defensive war was permitted. But even in the defensive war, the violence is restricted by Islam. In another Ayat, Holy Quran says,

"Allah forbids you not with regard to those who fight with you not for your Faith, nor drive you out of your homes, from dealing kindly and justly with them: for Allah loveth those who are just. Allah only forbids you with regard to those who fight with you for your Faith and drive you out of your homes, and support others in driving you out from turning to them for friendship and protection. It is such as turn to them in these circumstances that do wrong."[2]

The defensive war is permitted to help the helpless. In this regard, special instructions is also given. Holy Quran says,

"Let those fight for the cause of Allah who sell the life of this world for the Hereafter. To him who fighteth for the cause of Allah, whether he is slain or gets victory soon shall We give him a reward of great value. And why should ye not fight for the cause of Allah and of those who being weak are ill-treated and oppressed? Men, women and children whose cry is: "Our Lord! rescue us from this town whose people are oppressors; and raise for us from Thee one who will protect; and raise for us from Thee one who will help!" Those who believe in fighting for fight the cause of Allah and those who reject faith fighting for fight in the cause of evil: so fight ye against the friends of Satan: feeble indeed is the cunning of Satan."[3]

But, even in war, Muslims should not be negligent of discrimination and transgress. Quran says,

"O ye who believe! When ye go forth to fight in the way of Allah, be careful to discriminate, and say not unto one who offereth you peace: "Thou art not a believer;" seeking the chance profits of this life so that ye may despoil him. With Allah are plenteous spoils. Even thus, as he now is, were ye before; but Allah hath since then been gracious unto you. Therefore, take care to discriminate. Allah is ever informed of what ye do."[4]

"Fight for the cause of Allah with those who fight with you but do not transgress limits; for Allah loveth not transgressors."[5]

When the Holy Quran had given guidance as such, Mohammad, the Messenger of Allah, had fought 24 times with his enemies in the battlefields. None of those fights was meant for kingly power for the formation of royal kingdom, or for showing off a patriotic attitude. The Muslim armies were gathered for the defensive wars for the safety of believers. The bloodshed was done less. The number of martyred soldier in those 24 wars was 125 in all. The number of dead in the enemy army was 923. Many of them were killed due to natural calamities.

As per the instructions of Holy Quran, the main aim of those defensive wars was to protect the weak and innocent people who wanted to follow Islam, what they believe in, they were not fought for any land or property or power. Therefore, Mohammad, the Messenger of Allah, was used to giving strict instructions to Muslim soldiers prior to any battle.

"Don't use the weapon in war for violence only. A weapon is meant for self-defence. It is not meant for violence."

In the second year of Hijri, on the 17th day of Ramadan, the armies of pagan people of Makkah were to attack the army of Muslims at Badr. Before the war, Muslims were called for Salat. Mohammad, the Messenger of Allah, led the prayer. After the Salat, Mohammad, the Messenger of Allah, gave instructions to his soldiers,

"Remember, victory never depends either on the majority of soldiers, or on power or on might or on full supply of armaments. Victory depends on patience, confidence and the belief in Allah."[6]

The theosophical personality of Mohammad, the Messenger of Allah, was not separated from the administrator's personality of him. The two personalities were unique but one was in the Messenger of Allah. Whatever: Mohammad, the Messenger of Allah, had preached as the principles of Islam, he had kept those discourses in practice in his real day-to-day life sincerely. Thus, Mohammad, the Messenger of Allah, became a best model for Muslims in the society of pagans. He ran the administration of his Islamic society in righteous manner. He demonstrated the truth through his life that Islam was not full of violence, but full of peace, dedication, contribution and sacrifice of selfishness.

References

1. Holy Quran- 22- 39-40-41. Uzina lil lazina yuqa_talu_na bi an nahum zulimu_ wa in nal la_ha 'ala_ nasrihim laqadir. Nil lazina ukhriju_ min diya_rihim bigairi haq qin il la_ ay yaqu_lu_ rab bunal la_h wa laula_ daf'ul la_hin na_sa ba'dahum biba'dil lahud dimat sawa_mi'u wa biya'uw wa salawa_tuw wa masa_jidu yuzkaru fihas mul la_hi katsira_ wa layanshuran nal la_hu may yansuruh in nal la_ha laqawiy yun 'aziz. Al lazina im mak kan na_hum fil ardi aqa_mus sala_ta wa a_tuz zaka_ta wa amaru_ bill ma'ru_fi wa nahau anil munkar wa lil la_hi 'a_qibatul umu_r.

2. Holy Quran - 60- 8-9 - La_ yanha_kumul la_hu anil lazina lam yuqa_tilu_kum fid dini wa lam yuhkriju_kum min diya_rikum an tabar ru_hum wa tuqsitu_ ilaihim in nal la_ha yuhib bul muqsitin. In nama_ yanha_kumul la_hu anil lazina qa_talu_kum fid dini wa akhraju_kum min diya_rikum wa zaharu_ may yatawal lahum fa ula_ika humuz za_limu_n.

3. Holy Quran-4-74-75-76-Falyuqa_til fi sabililla_hil lazina yasyru_nal haya_tad 'dunya_ bill a_khirah(ti), wa may yuqa_til fi sabililla_hi fayuqtal au yaglib fasaufa nu'tihi ajran 'azima_(n). Wa ma_ lakum la_ tuqa_tilu_na fi sabililla_hi wal mustad'afina minar rija_li wan nisa_'i walwilda_nil lazina yaqu_lu_na rabbana_ akhrijna_ min ha_zihil qaryatiz za_limi ahluha_, waj'al lana_ mil ladunkawaliyya_(n), waj'al lana_ mil ladunka nasira_(n). Allazina a_manu_ yuqa_tilu_na fi sabililla_h(i), wallazina kafaru_ yuqa_tilu_na fi sabilit ta_gu_ti fa qa_tilu_ auliya_'asy syaita_n(i), inna kaidasy syaita_ni ka_na da'ifa_(n).

4. Holy Quran -4.94-Ya_ ayyuhal lazina a_manu_ iza_ darabtum fi sabililla_hi fa tabayyanu_ wa la_ taqu_lu_ liman alqa_ ilaikumus salama lasta mu'mina_(n), tabtagu_na'aradal haya_tid dunya_, fa'indalla_hi maga_nimu kasirah(tun), kaza_lika kuntum min qablu fa mannalla_hu 'alaikum fa tabayyanu_, innalla_ha ka_na bima_ ta'malu_na khabira_(n).

5. Holy Quran -2-190- Wa qa_tilu_ fi sabililla_hil lazina yuqa_tilu_nakum wa la_ ta'tadu_, innalla_ha la_ yuhibbul mu'tadin(a).

6. Shame-E-Feraza, by Mehboob Desai- Kusum Prakashan, Ahmedabad, p. 37.

6

Parable on Kurbani

Ajha. 'Ajha' means sacrifice, renunciation or abandonment. The festival expressing pleasure of sacrifice means Id-ul-Ajha. Id-ul-Ajha is also called 'Id-e-Kurban'; Id of sacrifice, Bakr-id or Kabir Id. The tale of sacrifice associated with this Id expresses the principle of all-around devotion of Islam.

Quran-e-sharif and Muslim historians present the unique tale of sacrifice connected with the sacrifice. Associated with that tale is a great prophet of Islam, Hazrat Ibrahim.

Ibrahim means Father of the people. Hazrat Ibrahim was a dear servant of God. Because of his closeness with God, only he was called 'Khalilullah', that is, dear friend of God. Hazrat Ibrahim's relation with God was like unique symbol of devotion and trust. Without disobeying a single command of God, Hazrat Ibrahim worshiped Him day and night. His such holy and immeasurable devotion made him the dear friend of God. God always tests His dear servants. According to such eternal truth, one day God decided to test His dear friend Hazrat Ibrahim.

The tale of this test is the heart of Id-ul-Ajha. This tale is given in 23rd para of 'Soorturassa fikali Ruku-between 101 and 107 commandments' of Quran-e-sharif.

Known as the Father of prophets Ibrahim used to pass through hard tests from the very childhood. As he did not agree with his father's improper ideas, he left his father's house at a very small age. While leaving the house and the native place, his words were :

'I go near my protector. He only will show the right path.'

And God agreed to bless him. He made him active on the path of worship. He emigrated from Babylone and settled in Haran. There he prayed to God one day :

'O my protector, give me one honest son.'

Thereafter he went to Egypt. After coming from that place, he lived in Rabran for ten years. Here he married to Hazrat Hajra. At that time, he begged for the same blessing. God fulfilled his this prayer at the age of eighty-six. Son was born at his place. He named him Ismail, means to say to God again and again. After many prayers by Hazrat Ibrahim Ismail was born. A son was born in his family. Ismail was born to him. His name was therefore quite proper. Hazrat Ismail was as God-worshipper and honest as his father. When Hazrat Ibrahim reached the age of moving about himself, that is, became eight to ten years old, he saw a dream one night. In the morning, Hazrat Ibrahim talked his dear son Hazrat Ibrahim about that dream.

'My son, I saw in the dream tonight that by the order of God, and on his name, I am sacrificing you.'

Son Ismail, too, was God-worshipper. Befitting an ideal son he said to his father humbly :

'Father, carry out literally the order which has been given by God in dream. God will give me the power of endurance at the time of sacrifice.'

After this talk between father and son, Hazrat Ibrahim said to his wife Hazrat Hazra :

'Today I am going to take Ismail out withme for some work. So prepare him.'

Without asking a single question, wife Hazrat Hazra accepted her husband's order over her head. She bathed her son Ismail, dressed him with new clothes and prepared him. And father and son both set off to obey God's command. They reached Meena which was five miles away from his tent.

We find in the record of Islamic literature that Satan made unlimited efforts to puff up mother, father and son so that God's order may not be carried out. But the title-bearer of 'Khalilullah' Hazrat Ibrahim, his honest son Ismail and wife Hazra—none of the three-even slightly wavered.

Hazrat Ibrahim reached on a hillock named 'Munhar'. Thinking that this is the best place for sacrifice, father looked at his dear son. Having sensed father's sight, the son, too, became ready for sacrifice. Hazrat Ismail laid his face on the ground, bent his neck and lay down on a stone. No sooner did Hazrat Ibrahim raise his knife to execute God's command till the end, than son Ismail said to his father :

'Dear father, tie a band round on your eyes so that son's love may not come in the way of obeying God's command.'

Father Ibrahim was highly pleased on seeing his son's devotion towards God, and he tied the band round his eyes. He, then, rolled his knife on his dear son, but the knife did not do its work. Saying 'O, the greatest God (Allah-u-Akbar), he rolled the knife again; but it did not work at all. At the same moment, a mystic voice hummed in the Munhar hillock.

'O Ibrahim, you have literally obeyed God's command. God tests his honest servants in this way only. You have passed through God's test. So, in stead of Ismail, you sacrifice an animal as a symbol.'

And Hazrat Ibrahim accordingly for the first time sacrificed (*i.e.* killed) the animal at the place called Meena located on the hillock named Munhar, to carry out God's command.

From this day onwards, the custom of sacrificing some animal in the name of God began.

In this story given in Quran-e-Sharif, worship (ibadat) means Hazrat Ibrahim's faith in God. Sacred and real worship demands renunciation, abandonment and sacrifice. God took the test of Hazrat Ibrahim's true worship through this incident. It is also said in Quran-e-Sharif :

'Certainly, it was just a test.'

Accordingly, the main aim of the custom of sacrifice accepted in Islam is all-round devotion. The emphasis is laid on giving up the dearest thing or an individual for the sake of God. Through this kind of renunciation or sacrifice, one's faith towards God or worship is expressed. That is, sacrifice is the symbol of all-around devotion. It is, therefore, only said in Quran-e-Sherif :

'The meat or blood of sacrifice you offered does not reach till God, but what reaches Him is your faith and holy worship only.'

In Islam, four matters are accepted as duty : prayer, day fasting, giving alms and Hajj. A Muslim who goes for Hajj has to offer sacrifice to his companions during Hajj. But for any reason, if sacrifice be done during Hajj, its option has also been stated in Quran-e-Sharif :

'One who cannot do sacrifice should do three day fasting in the days of Hajj and seven day fastings after returning home.'

This matter suggests that the spirit behind sacrifice mainly is renunciation and abandonment and that is inevitable, too, to reach near God.

The tradition of offering sacrifice is woven with every religion. In the ancient and medival India, the custom of offering sacrifice to Gods and Godesses at the time of religious rites was prevalent in Hindu society. In ancient temples this custom remained in existence for a long time. Of course, behind that custom too, worship of Gods and Godesses was in the centre. From that point of view, in both

Hindu and Islam religions, the custom of sacrifice, in real sense, is associated with devotion of worship.

Renunciation or sacrifice is necessary even for the protection of human values. Its contribution even to sustain the existence of whole human society has remained noteworthy. Sacrifice given by Jesus Christ to convey God's message up to the people, world's first 'satyagrah' like Hazrat Husain's sacrifice, Shri Rama's sacrifice of throne to obey father's command, Gandhiji's sacrifice for the preservation of moral values – all these are well-known in history. It is a wrong belief that sacrifice can be given by great men and prophets only. For the welfare of human society, a scientist does sacrifice by experimenting his research on his own self. Likewise, an engineer, doctors, teachers or any common man, remaining within their own fields, can serve religion and society by sacrificing their labour, time and money. Our society has urgent need of such spirit. The tale of sacrifice of Hazrat Ibrahim, his son Ismail and wife Hazrat Hazra will continue to remain from that point of view a guide for the whole human society. May Almighty give us all guidance to put this tale of sacrifice into practice. We only pray for such blessing, Amen.

7

Kurbani and Non-violence

The episode of Prophet Ibrahim, peace be upon him, is given in the Holy Quran in the Surah As-Saffat, from Ayat No. 101 to Ayat No. 107. This episode is the basic source of Islamic tradition of sacrifice. As per this episode, after a long and unbroken service to Allah, Prophet Ibrahim, got a son at the age of 86 years. The son was named 'Ismail'. Prophet Ismail, was brought up with love and affection by his parents. When the son was 8 or 10 years old, Prophet Ibrahim, had a dream. In the dream, Prophet Ibrahim, was ordered to sacrifice his beloved son for the sake of his Allah. In such ways, Allah tests His believers.

As soon as he received the order of sacrifice from his Allah, Prophet Ibrahim, took his son Ismail, to a forest. Son Ismail, also willingly followed his father. He knew the order of his Allah and he requested his father to sacrifice him as per the order of his Allah. Prophet Ibrahim, took his son to a mountain, kept the head of his son on a stone, and he tried to cut off the throat of his son with a sharp Knife. At that moment, once again the Holy Allah spoke to him, "O Ibrahim!" You have already fulfilled the dream !" Then, God made Prophet Ibrahim, to sacrifice a ram instead of his son, Ismail. Since then, as a redemption of one's own sins, sacrifice of beloved animal has been adopted by the people of Book, *i.e.* Jews, Christians, etc. The very same tradition is adopted by Islamic believers, too. Holy Quran reads,

"The nonviolence of Mahavir is delicately intricate and divine, whereas the non-violence being adopted and practiced by Mahatma Gandhi is humane in nature. When compared to these two kinds of non-violence, the Islamic non-violence is innate, sensible and practical."

Once Gandhiji said,

"Many Muslim friends have told me that Muslims will not accept non-violence indiscriminately. As per their saying, for the Muslims, the violence is as righteous and necessary as non-violence. One of the two may be adopted as per one's need."[4]

For establishing the righteousness and equality of these two things there is no need of citations from Holy Quran. The creed of sacrificing animals is adopted by human race since the times immemorial. Moreover, nowhere in the world, there is any indiscriminate violence. Exactly opposite to it, I have heard from many of my Muslim friends that Holy Quran recommends practice of non-violence many a time. As per its instructions, patience and pardoning is more important than revulsion and retaliation.

References

1. Holy Quran- 37-101 to 107 - Fabas syarna_hu bighula_min halim. Falam ma_ balaga ma'ahus saya qa_la ya_ bunay ya in ni ara_ fil mana__mi an ni azbahuka fanzur ma_za_ tara_ qa_la ya_ abatifal ma_ tumaru satajiduni in sa_ al la_hu minas sa_birin. Falam ma_ aslama wa tal lahu_ liljabin. Wa na_daina_hu ay ya_ ibra_him. Qad shad daqtar ruya_ in na_ kaza_lika najzil muhsinin. In na ha_ za_ lahuwal bala_ ul mubin. Wa fadaina_hu bizibhin azim.

2. Holy Quran- 22-36-37- "Wal budna ja'alna_ha_ lakum min sa'a_ril la_hi lakum fiha_ khairun fazkurus mal la_hi 'alaiha_ sawa_f fa iza_ wajabat junu_buha_ fakulu_ minha_ wa at'imul qa_ni'a wal mu'tar kaza_lika sakh kharna_ha_ lakum la'al lakum taskurun. Lay yana_lal

la_ha luhu_muha_ wa la_ dima_ uha_ wa la Kiy yana_luhut taqwa_ minkum kaza_lika sakh kharaha_ lakum litukab birul la_ha 'ala_ ma_ hada_kum wa bas siril muhsinin."

3. Holy Quran-2-196- "Wa atimmul hajja wal 'umrata lilla_h(i), fa in uhsirtum famastaisara minal hady(i), wa la_ tahliqu_ ru'u_sakum hatta_ yablugal hadyu mahillah(u_), fa man ka_na minkum maridan au bihi azam mir ra'sihi fa fidyatum min siya_min au sadaqatin au nusuq(in), fa iza_ amintum, fa man tamatta'a bill 'umrati ilal hajji famastaisara minal hady(i), fa mal lam yajid fasiya_mu sala_sati ayya_min fil hajji wa sab'atin iza_ raja'tum tilka 'asyaratun ka_milah(tun), za_lika limal lam yakun ahluhu_ ha_diril masjidil hara_m(i), wattaqulla_ha wa'lamu_ annalla_ syadidul 'iqa_b(i)."
4. Harijan Bandhu- 8th August, 1939, p. 258.

8

Jihad and Non-violence

In the present times, the terrorists are using the word 'Jihad' for justifying their inhuman violence against their enemies. We know that no religion supports terroristic violence. Hence, no terrorist is a follower of any religion. A terrorist believes in his own narrow-minded. He joins his own type of terrorism to an ancestral religion.

The theosophical meaning of Jihad, that is, the real meaning of Jihad is not well-known to common people in our society. Jihad means to strive on the way to Allah with one's own life, means and measures to get His blessings. For achieving His mercy, one has to face the difficulties with patience, but not to create difficulties impatiently for others. Jihad means to strive. This can be any kind of striving on the way to God, which involves either spiritual or personal effort, material resources, or arms. Jihad is also used to refer to a war waged by the Muslims for the defence or advancement of Islam; its interests and ideals. In this regard, Mohammad, the Messenger of Allah, said,

"Strive against selfish desires and greediness."

"Let us be freed ourselves from little striving. In the little striving, Muslims shall have to fight with non-believers. It happens once in a while. Let us practice the great striving, that is against selfishness. Muslims shall have to exercise Jihad against selfishness."

The word striving or Jihad is used profusely in Holy Quran. But, in the whole of Holy Quran, the word 'Jihad' is not used in relation to indiscriminate war, innocent blood-shedding and indiscreet violence. As far as I know, in Arabic language, the word 'Jihad' means 'to strive; to attempt'. To strive on the way Allah is called Jihad in Islam. If one strives with all might and main to serve the poor people, feed the needy people, to restrain oneself, to pray consistently, to advise wisely, to guide others on right path, to make efforts for achieving righteous things, such things are called Jihad. Holy Quran says,

"Do Jihad with patience."

Word Jihad includes many righteous efforts of Muslims in the way of Allah. Many people of Makkah had migrated to Ethiopia, ruled by a Christian King, to safeguard their religion and their lives. It was also called Jihad by Mohammad, the Messenger of Allah. If a person served his old parents, his service was called Jihad. If a woman performed Umra or Hajj, the performance was called Jihad. Mohammad, the Messenger of Allah used Jihad in many contexts. While giving guidance to Mohammad, the Messenger of Allah, Allah says in Holy Quran,

"Fight those who believe not in Allah in nor (God) on the Last Day nor hold that forbidden which hath been forbidden by Allah and His apostle, nor acknowledge the religion of truth (even if it is) of the People of the Book until they pay the Jizya with willing submission and feel themselves subdued."[1]

This guidance is binding on all Muslims. Aisha, the Mother of Muslims (R.A. = Rahimtullah Alayahi) (RA) narrated,

"I said, "O Allah's Apostle! Shouldn't we participate in Holy battles and Jihad along with you?" He replied, "The best and the most superior Jihad for women is Hajj which is accepted by Allah." Aisha added: Ever since I heard that from Allah's Apostle I have determined not to miss Hajj."[2]

One day, a man asked Mohammad, the Messenger of Allah,

"Who is the best among Muslims?"

Mohammad, the Messenger of Allah, replied,

"One that strives on the way to Allah with all of his means and might."

The person asked for clarification,

"What does it mean?"

Mohammad, the Messenger of Allah, replied,

"One that strives on the way to Allah means one that fasts in the day time and performs Salat in the night time."[3]

Likewise, Abdullah Bin Mas'ud narrated,

"I asked Allah's Apostle, "O Allah's Apostle! What is the best deed?" He replied, "To offer the prayers at their previously stated fixed times." I asked, "What is next to goodness?" He replied, "To be good and dutiful to your parents." I further asked, what is next to goodness?" He replied, "To participate in Jihad for Allah's cause." I did not ask Allah's Apostle anymore and if I had asked him more, he would have told me more."[4]

Also, Abu Said narrated,

"Allah's Messenger was asked who would be most excellent and most exalted in degree in Allah's estimation on the Day of Resurrection, and he replied, "The men and women who make frequent mention of Allah." He was asked if they would be superior even to the man who had fought for Allah's cause. Allah's Messenger replied, "Even though he plied his sword among infidels and polytheists till it was broken and smeared with blood, the one who made mention of Allah would have a more excellent degree than he."[5]

Once one person asked Mohammad, the Messenger of Allah,

"Which is the best way of Jihad?"

Mohammad, the Messenger of Allah, replied,

"The best way of Jihad is to keep restraint on one's actions and to fight against one's own anger and greediness. That is the best way of Jihad."

In Islamic terminology, the best way of Jihad is called "Jihad E Akbari."

Thus, Jihad is not used only for war and blood shedding. Many a time, Jihad is used to indicate the striving and struggling on the way to Allah, without using any deadly weapons. Many a time, a striving and struggling with weapons is mentioned by 'Qatal' or 'Qatl' means 'to kill'.[6]

Even the word 'Qutal' is used few times in the Holy Quran, like in Surah Al Baqara and in Surah Al Israa. When the word Jihad indicates such beautiful meanings of theological status, it is not befitting to use Jihad for causing the unwanted terrorism and meaningless murders by some misguided people. When the people come to know about the difference between Jihad and qatl, the concept of Islam will take a new mode, then, the Critics will stop to relate the terrorism with Islam, the Peace.

References

1. Holy Quran - 9-29- Qa_tilul lazina la_ yu'minu_na billa_hi wa la_ bill yaumil a_khiri wa yuharrimu_na ma_ harramalla_hu wa rasu_luhu_ wa la_ yadinu_na dinal haqqi minal lazina u_tul kita_ba hatta_ yu'tul jizyata 'ay yadiw wa hum sa_giru_n(a).
2. Sahih al-Bukhari-3-84.
3. Gujarati Imam Bukhari Sharif - Part 11 to 15, p. 53-54.
4. Sahih al Bukhari- Hadith-4.41.
5. Al-Tirmidhi-Hadith-2278.
6. Hazarat Mohammad Ane Islam by Pundit Sunderlal, pp. 137-138.

9

Islam and Terrorism

The meaning of English word 'terror' is fear, danger or oppression. In Urdu, the word used for it is *'daheshat'*. In Urdu, the word terrorism is called *'daheshat pasand'* (which means someone liking, choosing or accepting 'terror'). There is not the slightest relation between Islam and terrorism, the word which is entwined with the meanings like fear, danger or violence. I don't feel any hesitation in saying that certainly Muslim 'Alims', 'maulavis' or intellectuals like me have failed in awakening that truth.

Islam and terrorism are quite opposite to each other. They cannot meet at the same place. Terror or violence which spreads in the name of Islam has not any relation with the basic principles of Islam. Islamic Sahitya Prakashan, Amdavad has published a booklet bearing the title : *Atankwad ane Islam*. This booklet is worth reading by everyone. It is written in that booklet :

"If some Muslims spread excitement through terrorism, it has no relation with Islam. This action would be considered rather like disrespect of Islamic religion, and conversion in 'Shariat-e-Muhammadi', which will be regarded a sign of discourtesy in the perspective of religion and 'shariat'. Islam does not permit to cause pain or corruption."

The word 'Islam' has come down from 'Arabic word: *sa* (स) *la* (ल) *ma* (म). The word *slim* (स्लिम) made with the letters of the root *'salama'* means ease and peace. In that sense, a few quotations are respectfully offered hereunder to the people who are strong supporters of peace, playing wild dance of violence in the name of Islam:

"The whole universe is the family of God. The most lovable person to God is the one, who behaves well with family."

"Then God will think about whoever does the slightest good, and also think about whoever does the slightest evil."

"Your God is not such that He may unnecessarily destroy the populace, especially when there are reformers among them."

"How is God concerned in unnecessarily causing you pain, provided you continue to show gratefulness and practice the conduct of religion ?"

"O messenger of God, we have sent you, making you kind for the world".

"Don't create quarrel on the earth, when there has already become improvement. And remember God with fear and greed certainly, God's favour is near the men of character."

"And if you take revenge on people, take it only that much as much you have been oppressed. But if you act with patience, certainly, it is extremely good for you."

"Crusade means to fight according to the path paved by God. God's path means the path of values and humanity."

"And in the path of God, fight with those people who fight with you, but do not exaggerate; God does not prefer the one who exaggerates."

Above commandments of Quran-e-Sharif express in clear words the power of endurance of Islam for all those who enjoy cruel joy by spreading terrorism in the name of Islam.

PART–2

10

Mohammed and Peace

Some one asked Gandhiji, "What is religious righteousness[1]?"

Gandhiji replied, "The Truth is God."

The truth means values, morality, and implementation of values, that is, the religious righteousness or dharma. In such implementation, peace and belief are involved. When one implements the values, it gives peace to oneself. Peace is the symbol of happiness. For the attainment of peace, there is no need to deject the worldly life. While living the normal worldly life, Ram Krishna, Jesus and Prophet Mohammad worshiped the Ishwar, God or Allah. They made their followers, experience the taste of peace.

With reference to the same meaning, the word 'Om Shanti' is originated in the religion of Hindus. While explaining the greatness of 'Om Shanti', Maharshi Arvind revealed,

> 'Om' is the signature of Supreme God, one's experience of Supreme God[2]. It is a way to attain the Supreme God. It is the representative of Supreme God. If one meditates on 'Om', one's troubles end, and one achieves the success in one's life.'

If the word 'Om' is prefixed with the word 'Shanti', it greatly heightens its value. The 'Om Shanti' contains the attainment of Supreme God, and it makes one experience the existence of Supreme God. Moreover, two types of peace is expected from it; firstly, the divine peace, and secondly, the earthly peace. The divine peace occupies the mind and spirit, whereas, the earthly peace is the result of attainment of physical pleasures.

The concept of peace in Islam is very similar to the concept of peace in the Hindu religion. The meaning of 'Islam' is peace, consultation, submission, life being controlled by God, constantly struggling on the right way of truth for manly attainments, to say it in devotional language, to submit one's everything to the Supreme God. The essence of all these meanings is 'the Truth' in Islam.

In Islam, when two persons meet, they greet with a prayer. They say, 'Asslam alaicum', *i.e.* "May peace be upon you." However, such interpretation of Islam is not well known in public. The so-called Muslims, who are sympathizing with terrorism, do not understand this interpretation very well. Prophet Mohammad was a beautiful model of 'patience' and 'peace'. When the age of darkness was overshadowing the Arab lands, there was a common tradition in the Arabs that they would bury their female child alive in the hot sands. While spreading the humanistic principles through Islam, Prophet Mohammad faced numerous difficulties, insults and hatred. Even then, the shining of peace - only peace spread on his countenance.

The Messenger of Allah, Mohammad used to say always, "La tu fasid." It means 'Do not make mischief. Do not act wickedly'.[4] During the whole life of Prophet Mohammad, not a single incident did happen where he used force, coercion, wickedness, undue influence or cruelty to spread the word of Allah. The Quran says "La_ ikra_ha fid din (i)".[5] It means, let there be no compulsion in religion. The Prophet Mohammad followed this divine instruction strictly. The life of Prophet Mohammad was full of peace, patience, and simplicity. On many occasions, he taught his followers about these subjects. We can see a number of those occasions in his life.

The day was 17th of Ramzan, 2 Hijri. The Battle of Badr would be taking place on that day. It was the first straight battle between the Muslims and unbelievers at Badr. It was a battle between Truth and Falsehood, between the faith in God and the irreverence to God. While Prophet Mohammad was preparing for the battlefield, he announced, 'Assalat ya ibadallah'. It means, "O worshippers of God! It is time for Salat[6]." As soon as Prophet Mohammad announced the timing of prayer, every Muslim did ablution to prepare for prayer. Every one gathered at a place. The Prophet Mohammad led the prayer. After finishing the prayer, he gave a short discourse on the importance of Jihad. He said,

> "Remember. Success does not depend on the mass of fighters, or on their social status, affluence, armoury, or on their arsenal. The real thing for the success in a battlefield is patience, stability and belief in Allah."

During the whole life of Prophet Mohammad, he had to fight on 24 occasions. The total number of martyrs in these battles were as few as 125. As many as 923 persons were killed on the side of unbelievers. Humanly unavoidable circumstances had made Prophet Mohammad participate in those battles. In every battlefield, he took the defensive steps only. He instructed his followers to use their arms only for their defence, and not to kill the enemy unnecessarily. Even his sword was engraved with beautiful words, such as "Forgive him who wrongs you; join him who cuts you off; do good to him who does evil to you; and speak the truth even if it be against yourself."[7]

To establish the concept of Islamic peace in the society, it is mandatory to establish equality among all persons. Inequality in the society among the human beings is the main cause for turbulence and terrorism. For establishing the just peace in the society, the Islam accepts the equality of all persons, irrespective of age, affluence, aborigine,

actions and to fight against one's own anger and greediness. That is the best way of Jihad."

In Islamic terminology, the best way of Jihad is called 'Jihad E Akbari'. So, those persons who are spreading terrorism in the name of Jihad, and those who are practicing the terrorism in the name of Allah, are in real sense, not Muslims. Neither they understand the concept of Jihad nor they are associated with real Jihad. In the shades of Islamic Jihad, they are nurturing the terrorism. The terrorism is the outcome of their mental imbalance rather than their belief in Islam. Due to their foolishness, numerous Muslims who are living peacefully along with non-Muslims are subjected to many hardships. The others are alienating the peaceful Muslims in their own native motherland. Due to these terrorists, others are forced to doubt the patriotic spirits of Muslim brethren in their native country. This tendency is increasing day by day. When the others are thinking that the Muslims are supporters of terrorism, the truth is, Islam never supported any kind of terrorism. It teaches peace, love, and mercy towards human beings, and even against flora and fauna. Messenger of Allah always loved to protect the lives of animals and birds.

Once, the Messenger of Allah and his companions were travelling. Abdullah Ibn Mas'ud narrated, "One day we saw a bird with her two young offsprings. We captured the two young offsprings. The bird came and began to spread its wings. The Messenger of Allah, came and said, "Who grieved this for its young ones? Return its young ones to it."[10]

Prophet Mohammad freed the young offsprings of the bird. They joined their mother. The mother bird and its offsprings were quivering with fear. The mother was trying to hide its offsprings under its wings. This plight of birds disturbed Prophet Mohammad. He said, 'Do you not sense the fear of these little birds and their mother? Go, and put them back in their own place safely."

Once Prophet Mohammad was going on his way. He saw a camel. It was very weak, looking like a living skeleton and unable to bear the burden. Even then, one person was riding on it. Prophet Mohammad gave advice to him, "How can you use this weak and mute animal? Fear Allah. Use it only when it is fit for riding."

When Islam preaches mercy and gentleness towards birds, animals and trees, then there is no scope for uproar, cruelty or terrorism. There are plenty of Ayats in Quran, which abundantly explain about mercy, gentleness, and non-violence and which make mandatory to implement them in practice by all Muslims. In fact, to know the real meaning of peace and non-violence, it is necessary to understand Islam in its true colours. Incomplete knowledge of Islam is creating antagonism against divinely-advised humane activities. The incomplete knowledge is creating psychologically weak and mentally wicked persons. Due to these few terrorists, the peaceful and gigantic Islam is getting a bad name unduly and unjustly.

Once someone asked Mr. Bernard Shaw, the famous critic, thinker and dramatist, "Which is the greatest religion in the world?" Mr. Bernard Shaw simply replied, "Islam." At the next moment, he finished his reply, "But the followers of Islam have not understood it properly. As a result, it is getting a bad name."

The followers of Islam are failing to spread the real meaning of Islam. As a result, the terrorists are spreading their ideology as a concept of Islam. Once the real Muslims, who endeavour to follow the tenants of Islam in real sense, can remove the misunderstanding of the world about Islam. As a follower of Islam, I pray to my God that

"O My God! Let every Muslim follow the tenant of Islam in practice. Let him be an icon to prove that the Islam is religion of humanity in the whole world. Amen."

References

1. Dharma.
2. Parmatma.
3. Peace be upon him.
4. Al Quran. Surah 2. Ayat -74: fazkuru_ a_la_'alla_hi wa la_ ta'sau fil ardi mufsidin (a). -so bring to remembrance the benefits (ye have received) from Allah and refrain from evil and mischief on the earth.
5. Al Quran. Surah 2. Ayat 256 - La_ ikra_ha fid din(i), qad tabayyana'r rusydu minal gaiy(i), famay yakfur bit ta_gu_ti wa yu'mim billa_hi fa qadistamsaka bil 'urwatil wusqa_ lanfisa_ma laha_, walla_hu sami'un 'alim(un) - Let there be no compulsion in religion. Truth stands out clear from error; whoever rejects evil and believes in Allah hath grasped the most trustworthy hand-hold that never breaks. And Allah heareth and knoweth all things.
6. Salat: prayer.
7. Hazarat Mohammad Ane Islam by Pundit Sunderlal - Nav Jivan Prakashan - Ahmedabad, pp. 37-38.
8. Purifying Tax (Zakat): This is an annual payment of a certain percentage of a Muslim's property, which is distributed among the poor or other rightful beneficiaries. The obligatory tax that every Muslim must give. It is one of the five pillars of Islam. The Zakat is used to provide for the poor and destitute.
9. Book 2 - Belief - 1.11. Sahih All Bukhari.
10. Sunan Abu Dawood-Hadith-2669.

11

Mohammed : An Ideal Father

We all know Hazrat Mohamed Paygambar (Prophet) as the re-creator of Islam, but Mohamed Saheb also lived a worldly life. The note of Hazrat Mohamed Saheb's role as a father, husband and grandfather has been taken everywhere in Islamic literatures. In it Mohamed Saheb has been beautifully drawn as an ideal father, best husband and lovable grandfather.

Mohamed Saheb's role as a father has remained very difficult. To know and enjoy Mohamed Saheb as a father showering his love upon his daughter Hazrat Fatima is an occasion of great pleasure. Against daughter's immeasurable love, Mohamed Saheb has never compromised with the rules and regulations of Islam, and yet he remained an ideal father.

If Mohamed Saheb had desired, he could have done Hazrat Fatima's (*'Rahemtulla Alayhi'*) marriage in a rich family of Arabia. But Mohamed Saheb gave importance to cultures and ideals of Islam rather than to wealth. And that, too, with the consent of Hazrat Fatima, one day when Hazrat Ali asked for maiden Fatima's hand, first of all, he considered it proper to understand daughter Fatima's wish as an ideal father. And he asked daughter Fatima :

"Dear daughter, what is your opinion about this relation?"

Hearing this question, daughter Fatima remained silent, but there was a smile of consent over her face. On seeing it, Mohamed Saheb said :

'Dear daughter Fatima, in your silence, I can see your willingness.'

And thus, with the sum of four hundred *'Miskal Mihar'* (about one hundred and eight rupees). Hazrat Ali and Hazrat Fatima were married. Mohamed Saheb himself read the *'Khutbo'* (prayer) of marriage. About this Mohamed Saheb has said :

'I am ordered by the Almighty that I should get Fatima's marriage with Ali done. Making you all witness I say that I have got Fatima's marriage done with Ali in exchange of four hundred 'Miskal Mihar'.

After marriage, just as a father bids good-bye to his daughter with a sorrowful heart, in the same way, Mohamed Sabeb had gone to bid good-bye to his daughter upto the door of his house with a heavy heart, and before bidding good-bye he had kissed the forehead of daughter Fatima and said:

'Now, both of you may go to your house.'

At the time of giving farewell to his daughter Fatima, he gave only eleven things. They included a cot woven with leaves of date-tree, a leather bed which was filled with leaves of date-tree, two water pitchers, two earthen bowls, a leather bag to fill water, one *'masalla'* (a carpet used at the time of prayer) one rosary and one mill of stone to grind flour.

On the next day of the farewell, Mohamed Saheb went to meet his dear daughter Fatima at her house. Standing outside the door, father asked for permission to enter his daughter's house. Hearing father's voice, daughter Fatima rushed to the door. Mohamed Saheb embraced his daughter. He then asked her to fetch water in a vessel. He then wetted both his hands in it. Thereafter he sprayed water upon his son-in-law Hazrat Ali first. Then he rolled that wet hand on daughter Fatima's head and said:

'Fatima, I have done your marriage with an individual who is the highest and reputed person of his noble family.'

And putting his other hand on Hazrat Ali's he said:

'Ali, your wife is one of the best women and is a piece of my heart.'

And the wetness of Mohamed Saheb is throat surged into his eyes, and quite silently, he left, and came out of his daughter's house.

After marriage, daughter Fatima had kept in centre his father's pieces of advice. Once Hazrat Ali returned home from travel very tired and said:

'I feel hungry. Give me to eat whatever food is there in the house.'

Hazrat Fatima said:

'For the last three days, there is not a single grain of barley in the house.'

Hazrat Ali was surprised, "Why did you not tell me?" He asked.

Hazrat Fatima replied:

'It is my father's advice: never trouble husband with problems.' And that's why lady Fatima used to do all household work herself, like to fill water, clean utensils and grind flour. At times while grinding it, her hands bruised, and yet she was doing her household work with patience. Taking pity of his wife, once Hazrat Ali said to Mohamed Saheb:

'Fatima gets very tired while doing household work. If you give one of the maid servants who has come in the form of goods of gifts, it would give some relief to Fatima in her work.'

Mohamed Saheb said peacefully:

'At present, four hundred propagandists of Islam have come in 'Masjid-e-Nabwi. They cannot be spared from their service'. And Hazrat Ali became quiet.

Such transparent and real love of father and daughter is an ornament of Islam.

12

Mohammed : An Ideal Husband

Hazrat Mohamed Paygamber* had married ten times (*i.e.* ten marriages) during his life-span of 61 years. Except his first marriage with Hazrat Khadija (596 A.D.) other marriages had been done because of political and social inevitability. An English historian Stanley Lanpol writes about this:

'The aim of remaining marriages was only political, that is, to tie the chieftains opposite to one another's parties in a single thread.'

In spite of this, Mohamed Saheb is practice, behaviour and love with each wife was equal. During Mohamed Saheb's whole life nowhere can be seen bitterness or inequality with any of his wife.

Mohamed Saheb is first marriage had taken place with Hazrat Khadija*. Hazrat Khadija was fifteen years older than Mohamed Saheb yet Mohamed Saheb is relation with her was loving and trustworthy. Hazrat Khadija was the very first individual who had accepted Islam by putting trust for the first time in Mohamed Saheb. The initial days of Islam were very hard. People used to hate and threaten to kill Mohamed Saheb. At such critical time Hazrat Khadija courage was the only greatest force. At such time, Hazrat Khadija used to say to Mohamed Saheb :

•(p.b.u.h.) = peace be upon him.

"O, the crown of my head, there is no risk over your life. God will never allow you to be insulted. You are even the discharger of the rights of relatives. You are the lifter of people's burdens. You help the poor and the needy. You treat the guests with full hospitality. That's why, God will protect you."

From the age of 25 to 50 years, Mohamed Saheb had spent life with the single wife Hazrat Khadija. His that married life was ideal. Historian Stanley Lanpol writes about this:

"Mohamed Saheb lived loyally with the wife who was older than he. Even when his wife was 65 years old, he used to love her as much as he loved her at the time of marriage. During those twenty-five years, never was heard a single breath against the good conduct of Mohamed Saheb."

After the death of Hazrat Khadija Mohamed Saheb did nine marriages during the last thirteen years. He did all those marriages with reference to only social and political problems and organization. After the death of Hazrat Khadija, Mohamed Saheb did second marriage with Hazrat Aysha, the daughter of his life-long companion Hazrat Abu Bakr. At that time, Aysha was 18 years old.

The climax of Mohamed Saheb is understanding could be seen in this: Mohamed Saheb who lived with understanding and love for twenty-five year older wife Hazrat Khadija, became successful as an ideal husband by reaching at the mental level even with Hazrat Aysha who was far younger than he. The basic reason behind it was Mohamed Saheb's frank and affectionate love which was above egoism. Even though he possessed the title of the Emperor of Arabia, Mohamed Saheb's simplicity and natural behaviour was admired by all his wives.

Mohamed Saheb always used to behave with his wives with a loving and smiling face. He used to assist his wife in household work. When his wife was kneading flour, Mohamed Saheb was giving her water. Sometimes, he used to fetch firewood for the stove. If she knitted bands of cot ever became loose, he at once started pulling and making them tight. He paid particular attention to the mood and anger of his wives.

Once Hazrat Aysha told Mohamed Saheb sarcastically:

"You claim that you are the messenger of God!"

On hearing Aysha's words, Mohamed Saheb laughed and said, continuing to laugh:

'I exactly know, Aysha, your pleasure as well as displeasure both.'

'How?' asked Hazrat Aysha.

Mohamed Saheb said:

"When you are pleased, you say. 'Oath of Mohamed's God', and when you are displeased, you say, 'Oath of Ibrahim's God.' "

On hearing Mohamed Saheb is story, Hazrat Aysha became very light and said:

'Certainly, God's messenger, you have rightly said. When I am displeased, I don't take your name.'

It is very difficult to get an example of Mohamed Saheb's equal relations with his wives during his whole lifetime. Mohamed Saheb has often said about relations with one's wife in his preachings, too:

'If a Muslim prepares a morsel with his own hands, and puts it into his wife's mouth, that too, has its value.'

The wife of Hazrat Unus was very hot-tempered. Once she misbehaved with Hazrat Unus in public. Everyone was surprised at it. On seeing it, Mohamed Saheb laughed, and said:

'What is worth surprising in it? To bear patience towards wife's impoliteness is also a crusade! It has plenty of value.'

At the time of Hazrat Khadija's death, Mohamed Saheb was extremely sad. At that time, lady Halhar, Hazrat Badim's sister, told Mohamed Saheb giving consolation:

'Why do you become so sad at such an old woman's death?'

Mohamed Saheb then, said in a sad note:

'When people hated me, she gave me love and courage. When no one helped me, Khadija was my real sympathizer.'

And with these words, Mohamed Saheb broke down.

There is no lack of men in the world enjoying the status of a husband, but forgetting the status of God's messenger and the emperor of Arabia, Hazrat Mohamed 'Paygamber' was, and will remain, the only one, to live as a common, and yet, an ideal husband.

13

Mohammed : An Ideal Commander-in-Chief

Mohamed Saheb p.b.u.h. = peace be upon him was not only *an ideal religious propagandist*, but he was also the best commander-in-chief and possessed the knowledge of war strategy. His such skill is expressed in all the battles that came to his lot during his life. As a commander-in-chief his battles were not destructive, but they were defensive. The words engraved on the handle of his sword make it clear :

> 'Forgive him who does injustice to you, associate with him who separates you from him, do good to him who does wrong to you, and always speak the truth, even though it may go against you.'

Acquaintance with the war Mohamed Saheb had only when he was just eight years old. In the history of Arabia, Mohamed Saheb, was the witness of 'Harb-e-Fijar' which means unholy war. In this long war Hazrat Mohamed Saheb had done the work of supplying arrows to his uncle.

Thereafter, Mohamed Saheb spent fifty-five years in the propaganda and spread of Islam. At the age of fifty-five, Mohamed Saheb had to face the war. Mohamed Saheb had established the empire in Madina, 286 miles away from Mecca. Kuraishes of Mecca started efforts to crush that empire. Mohamed Saheb did not pay attention to such small efforts of the inhabitants of Mecca, but one day, Kuraishes attacked on Madina with 700 camels, one hundred horses and one thousand selected soldiers. Mohamed Saheb, then, had no other go, but to ask for God's permission for this war. In connection with his that prayer, he received command through the God's message. Which exists in Quran-e-sharif even to-day as their testimony. God has said therein:

'Would you not fight with the people who themselves started the war?'

'And what has happened to you that you don't fight according to God's path for the protection of the weak, women and children?'

Having received such command of God, Mohamed Saheb set off for the defensive war with only 313 soldiers. This war was fought in 624 A.D. in the green valley called 'Badra'. It is, therefore, known as 'Jung-e-Badra', that war of Badra, in Islamic history.

Before the beginning of war, as befitting to a value-based warrior, Mohamed Saheb had ordered the soldiers before giving the key of success in war:

> 'Remember, of weapons and inexhaustible means and materials, what is most important thing for victory is patience, firmness and trust in God.'

Like the war of Kurukshetra, in this war, too, very close relatives stood face to face e.g. against Hazrat Umar Faruq, his maternal uncle was in Kuraish's army; against Hazrat Abu Bakr was his own natural brother Akil, against Abu Hoo Zaifar was his father Utlah Bin Rabih and brother Valid Bin Rabih. Abul Aaz himself who was Mohamed Saheb's son-in-law was in Kuraish's army, and that's why, even before the war, Mohamed Saheb had made efforts of compromise, but Kuraish army was full of egoism of its strength and its arms and ammunition. Before the starting of war, Mohamed Saheb had also referred about this while doing prayer:

> 'God, these Kuraishes are coming with the ego about their army and means and materials. There is no limit to their egoism. They oppose God. Please send us thy help'.

Before the war, Kuraish's army of one thousand soldiers had taken position at strategic point on the battle ground of Badra. The place where they had camped was smooth land. There were dust and earth on it. This helped easy movement of the army. Mohamed Saheb's is army's camp was on sandy land. This made the army's movement very difficult. There was no well or water stream nearby. So the problem was harassing them. Mohamed Saheb was the best war strategist. He changed the army camp at the last moment. He shifted his army to the place higher than Kuraish's army. There was full water facility. Being the higher place, it was possible to see the movement of Kuraish's army. Mohamed Saheb gave the code word to his army at the last moment. Ibn Isquah writes about this:

> 'In the war of Badra, Mohamed Saheb had given the code word 'shiar' (which means 'practice') to his army.'

Such code word had been used to make a sudden attack on the enemy or to identify his soldiers.

Before the starting of the war, Mohamed Saheb had ordered to the soldiers who had already stood in line as the last command:

> 'The beginning of the war shall not be made from our side; oppose the enemy only then when they make an attack.'

With such value-based skilful warfare of Mohamed Saheb and with God's favour, only 313 soldiers proved very hard for the army of one thousand soldiers of Kuraish. Moreover, God sent rain at the very time of war'. So, in the lower part where Kuraish's army had camped, water had collected there, causing dangerous disorder. And Mohamed Saheb, without drawing a single drop of blood, won the war.

In those days, there was a rule to kill the prisoners of war or to keep them as slaves, according to the rules of the war. But Mohamed Saheb created a new history by practicing full humanitarian behaviour with the prisoners of war. Among the prisoners of war those who were poor and helpless were set free by taking their promise not to fight against Muslims hereafter. Some capable and rich prisoners were set free by taking compensation from them, whereas educated prisoners of war were sentenced to make the illiterate Muslims literate. A punishment like a literate prisoner to teach ten illiterate Muslims—such punishment with reference to prisoners of war could be the first one in the history of the world. As long as all the prisoners of war remained under the protection of Mohamed Saheb, they were treated like guests.

We know Hazrat Mohamed 'Paygamber' as only the re-creator of Islam, but his evaluation in depth as a value-based commander-in-chief remains yet to be done.

14

Hazrat Imam Hussein

In every religion, there has been struggle between truth and untruth, morality and immorality, religion and irreligion. In Hindu religion battlefield of Kurukeshtra was the place of struggle and in Islam, place of Karabala is well known for the same intention. In the second chapter of the "Geeta" Lord Shri Krishna addresses Arjuna,

"Let there be kinsmen like Bhishma, Drona, yet standing by the religion, your duty is nothing else but to fight like a Kshatriya (a member of the warrior caste).

The battle of Karabala in which Hazrat Imam Hussein became martyr was not against the followers of different religions and foreigners, but it was against those who followed the same religion, and against the relatives of the same family; it was the battle between truth and untruth and immorality.

When Hazrat Imam Hussein marched towards *Kufa* to save Islamic kingdom of the tyrranies of Yazeed with his 72 companions, one follower, stopping him, said,

"Yazeed will certainly kill you, too".

At that time without showing any anger over his face, Hazrat Imam Husain had suddenly said,

"Only God's will be done".

Karabala's battle means the consequences of stopping Yazeed's efforts - Yazeed who controlled Islamic state through immoral path, quite contrary to the moral principles such as free elections, parliamentary system, freedom of expression, responsibility towards God and people, good use of public funds, rule according to

Quran-e-Sharif and justice. It was not, however, even battle in the real sense. In a battle, terrible destruction can be seen on both the sides, whereas seventy-two companions of Hazrat Imam Hussein were followers of non-violence. Before the battle Imam Hussein had said in sermon,

"This battle is not aggressive, but defensive."

and that is why, even Gandhiji has given Hazarat Imam Hussein the title of the ***"First Satyagrahi"*** of the world.

Hazrat Fatema, the daughter of paygambar Hazrat Mohammed saheb and son-in-law Hazrat Ali's son Hazrat Imam Hussein was born in Munnavar-e-Madina on the 5^{tn} Shaban (the eighth month) on 4th the Hijri year, (the year reckoned with the time Hazrat Mohammed Sake left Mecca for Medina).

The worship and charity of Hazrat Imam Hussein, who was brought up with extreme caressing by enjoying gambol in grand-father Mohammed paygemaber's lap is well-known for his worship and charity in the history of Islam. Someone asked once Hazrat Zaynul Abedin about Hazrat Imam Hussein who performed Hajj on foot twenty-five times.

"How is it that Hazrat, Imam Hussein has minimum progeny?"

The reply was "Because he used to engross himself day and might in God's worship Charity of *Hazrat* Imam also was spread far and wide. He was helping the old, weak and respectable people as much as they demanded. He used to give one thousand dinars and one thousand goats to the unemployed without any hesitation. Once a poor but respectable man came at his door. He sent a note,

"I am very poor. I have not money to buy even a single grain of barley. I have only one thing with me, and that is my credit. I have come to sell it to you. I agree to whatever value you may rate for it".

On reading this note Hazrat Imam Hussein rushed out of the home. Putting ten thousand ***'Diharam'*** in his hand and said,

"O requester, I am not able to manage at present more than this much amount, but you believe that you have not requested and I have not rated your credit".

Such noble and charitable was the nature of *Hazrat* Imama Hussein who always remained engrossed in God's worship. He remained the same even when he was surrounded by the enemy with his seventy-two companions.

Hazrat Imam Hussein and his seventy-two companions from surrounded the very first day of Muharram the place of ***Karabala.*** The young and old everyone were pining for a single drop of water on the seventh, eight and the ninth day of Muharram. The night between the ninth and the tenth day was the night of slaughter preceding Muharram. On that night four thousand cavaliers of Yazeed surrounded 72 companions of Imam Hussein who was like a worshipper of non-violence. At that time even, in order to stop violence, while surrendering himself, Hazrat Imam Hussein sent a message with Yazeed's companion,

"Kill me or imprison me, (if you want) but do not kill my innocent companions children and women"

But cruel Yazeed did not accept his plea and let loose his vast army on Imam Hussain's companions who valiantly opposed them. In that battle between truth and untruth, religion and irreligion, morality and immorality even 72 companions of Hazrat Imam Hussein proved too difficult to the huge army of Yazeed. Yazeed had to retreat and he was excited thereby. Neglecting all the rules and regulations of war, he started without any restraint, so much so that he wounded from behind the back with a blow even Hazrat Hussein who was sitting in the open (listening to a discourse), and thus Hazrat Imam Hussein and his companions became martyrs. That day was Friday, the tenth day of Muharram. The followers of Islam observe mourning as a mark of Martyrdom of Hazrat Imam Hussein who became martyr on the tenth day of October, 680 A.D. and Hijri 61.

'Muharram' is the first month of Hijri era. The new year begins with this month only. Muharram is an Arabic word, but after the martyrdom of Hazrat Imam Hussein the original meaning of Muharram has changed. Muharram means mourning or sorrow, such a meaning is in vogue at present and that is why Muslims do not arrange auspicious occasions like betrothal or marriage. The custom of taking out procession of 'Tajiya' (i.e. coffin made of bamboo sticks and paper carried in a precession during Muharram) on the ninth or tenth moon or day of Muharram is familiar. However, no such custom was in vogue till years after the martyrdom of Hazrat Imam Hussein. The tradition of talking out 'Tajiya' started in India since the period of emperor Taimur lang (i.e. lame). Tajiya is the symbol of Hazrat Imam Hussein's tomb. Tajiya procession, in its real sense, is a mourning procession. But in the absence of the real understanding behind it, we have inadvertently given it the form of festival. Let all of us, understanding the real significance of that mourning procession, and dealing it with proper behavior and practice, deserving its dignity, offer real homage, to Hazrat Imam Hussein and his companions.

15

Khilafat and Khalifa

15.1 Khilafat: An Ideal Rule

The system of rule of ancient India was based on the principles of Hindu religion. During the monarchy of that period, the king used to rule according to the principles of religion. Its best example was King Ram. Similarly, in Arabia, Islamic empire was set up by Hazrat Mohamed Paygambar *(p.b.u.h.). After Mohamed Saheb's death (632 A.D.) Islamic empire had begun.

'Khalifa' is an Arabic word. Its meaning is 'successor'. After the death of Mohamed Saheb, first of all Hazrat Abu Bakr (R.A.) was appointed on the rank of Mohamed Saheb's successor as 'Khalifa Rasullah' for the political and administrative management of Islamic empire. The administration which was established by 'Khalifa' is called 'Khilafat'. In English the word 'Khalifa' is written as 'Calif' or 'Khalifah' in both the ways. Thereafter this word became so prevalent that after 1258 A.D. it had been used even for the rulers of Baghdad.

In the rule of the state, just as monarchy, democracy, presidentship, dictatorship, and similar systems of rule are familiar, in the same way, 'Khilafat' is also a system of rule. It runs according to the commands of Quran-e-Sharif and the ideals percolating through the life-story of Mohamed Saheb. All the four Khalifas - Hazrat Abu Bakr, Hazrat Umar, Hazrat Usman and Hazrat Ali - selected as Khalifas, were the followers of Mohamed Saheb. They were his close followers.

---

*p.b.u.h. = peace be upon him.
*(R.A.) = *'Rahemtullah Alayahi'*

That's why Khilafat rule is very far away from anarchy or dictatorship. Features of democracy can be seen therein. But democracy does not mean mobocracy. All the four Khalifas cleary believed in it. During the rule of Hazrat Umar-Majils-e-Shoora, that is, Ministerial council, was in existence: This ministerial council took decision about small or big, all the problems relating to the state after consultation. Such 'Majils-e-Shoora' was in the centre and the state both. They can be compared with our Lok Sabha (House of Commons) and the Legislative Assembly. Members of the 'Majils-e-Shoora', however, were not the representatives of any party, race or class. They therefore took decisions in the interest of the state only disregarding their own interests.

When decision regarding any national or state problem is to be taken, the decision was taken jointly by the learned, and experienced representatives of the respective fields.

During the Khilafat rule, the nation was divided into province, district and taluka. During the period of Hazrat Umar the whole Islamic nation was divided into eight provinces - Mecca, Madina, Syria, Jajira, Basra, Kufa, Misra, and Falistin. With the expansion of Islamic state's area, other three provinces were added therein Khurasan, Ajarbaijan and Faras – the highest officer of each province was 'Wali' (Governor). In addition, other officers such as 'Sahibul Biraj', that is, collector, 'Sahibe Ahdas' that is, Police Officer, 'Sahibe Beytulmal'; that is, Finance officer, 'Kazi'; that is, Judge, were there. Every citizen had the right to complain against any officer – right from the Khalifa to the smallest officer. Once a citizen said to Hazrat Umar in public: 'O Umar, fear Allah'.

Before that citizen may speak anything more, an officer stopped him. 'Don't speak like this against Khalifa'.

Khalifa Umar, then, stopping him (the officer) said, 'Let him say whatever he wants to say. If he does not say fearlessly, he is not a real citizen, and if I don't hear him with the ease of mind, I am not a real Khalifa.'

Appointment of the Governors of states was made on the basis of thorough qualifications. Before accepting the ranks, the governor who was appointed had to take oaths which were led by the following matters :

1. 'I will not ride a Turky horse.'
2. 'I will not put on such clothes which may expose my body.'
3. 'I will not eat sieved flour.'
4. 'I will not keep a door-keeper or a watchman at the door of my house or office.'
5. 'I will always keep the doors of my house or office open for the needy people.'

15.2 Justice in Khilafat Rule

I continue to enjoy the nearness of Puri, the city of Orissa from where the beginning of historic pilgrimage of Jagannathjee has been. I go on writing this chapter, sitting in the institute of Gandhi Ashram Foundation (Pratisthan) situated at the far end of Puri. Just in front of me the beautiful sea-coast of Puri goes on roaring like a mischievous girl. And the picture of Jagannathjee's temple which I saw only yesterday rises before my eyes. The construction of Jagannathjee temple was done by king Anantbhim Dev in the 12th century. The temple is about eight hundred years old, and its architecture and art belong to Kalinga style. The temple has four parts: 'Viman' (the place where the idol of deity is kept, with a dome on it), 'Jagmohan' (probably, the open space in the temple before the idol where the worshippers collect), 'Natyamandal' (the place where the worshippers present performances), and 'Bhogmandal' (the space where 'prasad' is served.)

Such architectures and value-based ideas of Indian culture only have protected civilization and culture of India.

To sustain existence of Islam also contribution of its value-based ideas and architectures is remarkable. Khilafat rule is its best example. Its administration of justice and martial arrangement bear its witness even today.

In Khilafat rule, administration of justice was totally independent from general administration. Judicial procedure beginning from Khalifa to Kazi (*i.e.* judge) was running impartially. Appointment of Kazi, *i.e.* judge was made completely on the basis of merit, procedure for the judges appointed was prescribed. An order was notified in the name of Kufa's governor Hazrat Abu Musa Ashari, in which the procedure for judges was given. It was written therein :

(1) Kazis have to practice uniform behaviour with every small and big, rich and poor persons.

(2) In order to prove his complaint, a complainant only will have to present witnesses and supporting documents. If he is not able to present witness to prove his complaint, he will have to present his complaint on the oath of Quran-e-Sharif.

(3) The judge (Kazi) can get the compromise done between both the parties, but a law-suit in which the breach of the state's law is likely to be commited, compromise would not be possible in it.

(4) The Kazi can reconsider the judgement even after it has been declared.

(5) The date of conducting the law-suit will be decided with the consent of both the parties.

(6) If the complainant does not remain present after the fixation of the date, Kazi can give the judgement ex-parte.

(7) Every Muslim is eligible to give witness. But a Muslim who is sentenced or is proved guilty of giving false evidence cannot give witness anymore. In

Khilafat administration, in order to run the administration of justice in a clean and strong manner, following four matters had been accepted :

(a) Thorough clarification in the laws based on Quran-e-Sharif, so that the Kazi may not find any trouble or hesitation in arriving at the decision.

(b) Appointment of impartial and qualified officers only in the administration of justice.

(c) Strict execution of laws and rules. Administration of justice should be kept completely away from evils like nepotism, corruption, etc.

(d) Every year appointment of judges should be made in proportion to population so that no citizen may have to suffer delay in getting justice.

Equality was inevitable in the administration of justice. There were no differences like gentleman and a wicked person, rich and poor, king and the people in the administration of justice.

Once a dispute about something arose between Khalifa Hazrat Umar and Hazrat Ubai Bin Kaba. Hazrat Ubai Bin Kaba filed a law-suit in the court of Jed Bin Sabit. In that law-suit Khalifa Hazrat Umar was the accused. At that time, Judge Jed-Bin Sabit stood up, welcomed Khalifa Umar and said: 'Sitting arrangement can be made in the accused's box for you as an accused. You can sit and reply.'

Hazrat Umar said: 'I have not come here as Khalifa. I have presented myself before you as an accused. I am not, therefore, entitled to any such facility.'

15.3 Khalifa Hazrat Abu Bakr

The life of the first Khalifa of Islamic state (Ruler), Hazrat Abu Bakr (573-634 A.D.) was a noble example of simplicity, good conduct and truth. Hazrat Abu Bakr who was younger than Hazrat Mohamed Paygambar by three years, had unbreakable faith in Hazrat Mohamed Paygambar yet his faith in God's Paygambar originated from the time when he (*i.e.* Mohamed Saheb) was not Paygambar.

When the first message of God came down over Hazrat Mohamed Saheb, Abu Bakr was in Yemen for the business. At that time nobody was ready to believe Mohamed Saheb's story. When Abu Bakr returned from Yemen, he heard the story of the message (of God). Without thinking even for a single moment, he accepted Islam, believing Mohamed Saheb God's paygambar. Thus Abu Bakr was the first great man of the age to accept Islam, and he, therefore, received the second name (alias) of 'Siddique', meaning one who speaks truth. When Mohamed Saheb emigrated from Mecca to Madina (622 A.D.) he was with him then also. In Madina, it was he only who was the chief adviser of Mohamed Saheb.

Abu Bakr who had given concrete form to Mohamed Saheb's life-story and the principles of Islam, was an ideal example of simplicity and naturalness. Before he became Khalifa, he used to move from lane to lane of Mecca as a cloth merchant. He earned his living by loading a bundle of cloth on his shoulder and selling it from street to street. Every morning he milked his own goats as well as goats of his neighbours, and then he took them to graze. This was his daily routine. When Hazrat Abu Bakr became Khalifa, the most displeased person was a girl:

'Now who will milk my goats?

Who will take them to graze?'

These words reached Khalifa Hazrat Abu Bakr. He called that girl near him and said:

'I solemnly swear, I will always milk your goats and will take them to graze, too. The title of Khalifa will never keep me away from people's service.'

Hazrat Abu Bakr's reign as a Khalifa (632-634 A.D.) was impartial, friendly and humanitarian. It was during his reign only that Quran-e-Sharif was compiled and it received the form of a book. Commandments of Quran-e-Sharif on leather stones and those which were memorized were collected. It was arranged according to the titles and sequence given by Mohamed Saheb and its one copy was prepared in a book-form.

Besides this, his behaviour with non-Muslims, too, was human. Khalifa Abu Bakr had protected the rights and religious beliefs by notifying an order. It was stated therein:

> 'Religious places of non-Muslims should always be well protected. Their forts should not be destroyed, in which they take shelter to save themselves from the enemy at the time of war. They are completely free to play conch and bell at their religious places. They are permitted to move out in procession with the cross during the days of festivals.'

In the preachings of Hazrat Abu Bakr, fear of Allah was always expressed. He used to say:

'In every condition, fear from the Allah, Allah knows your deeds.'

Once Hazrat Abu Bakr was taken ill. He worried about the life after death as much as the worldly life. He, therefore, inquired:

'How much money have I withdrawn from State Exchequer as a Khalifa?' He received the reply: 'One thousand 'Dihrum' (about Rs. 1500/-).

Khalifa at once ordered: 'Credit that money in State Exchequer by selling my personal land.'

'After becoming Khalifa how much increase has been in my personal property?' The reply was: 'A negro slave, two camels and a bed-sheet.'

And at the same time Khalifa Abu Bakr made a will: 'After my death all this property may be handed over to the next Khalifa.'

When Hazrat Umar who was to become the second Khalifa, heard these words, he said in a mournful voice 'O Abu Bakr, you have left very hard duties for your successor.'

Hazrat Abu Bakr's daughter Hazrat Aisha, was the wife of Hazrat Mohamed Paygambar. Before death, he asked his daughter Aisha, 'How many clothes had been used to make the coffin of Mohamed Saheb?'

'Three clothes'; said Hazrat Abu Bakr.

'Make the coffin of three clothes – two cloth-sheets which are there on my body and one new cloth.'

Hearing this Hazrat Aisha spoke:

'Reverent father, we are not so poor that we can't bring a new cloth for coffin.'

Abu Bakr, then, said this much only,

'Dear child, new clothes are more suitable for living human beings than for dead body.'

One day Hazrat Mohamed Paygambar asked his companions: 'Who has observed Roza (day fasting) today?'

'I', (said Abu Bakr)

Mohamed Saheb asked again. 'Today who has given shoulder to the coffin? Who has served food to the poor? Who has gone to inquire about the health of the sick?' It was Abu Bakr only who gave affirmative reply to all these questions. Then Mohamed Saheb said:

'One who has done so many pious deeds in a single day will certainly go to heaven.'

Such value-based and bearing good conduct, the first Khalifa of Islam, Hazrat Abu Bakr, passed away on 23rd of

August, 634 A.D. According to Mohamed Saheb's statement, he would be spreading even today the bright light of Islam in heaven. Amen!

15.4 Khalifa Hazrat Umar

Hazrat Umar, whose original name was Umar Ibna Al Khatab, was born in the eighth generation of Hazrat Mohamed paygambar. He was born in Mecca in Kuresh family in 586 A.D. In youth proficient in wrestling and horse-riding, Hazrat Umar's bodily height was wonderful. His power of memory was amazing. He had memorized poems of high-calibered poets of that period. He was unique in remembering lines of dynasty. During his very young age he had established his name as a very good orator. Temperamentally, he was very hard and full of anger. That's why when he became Khalifa he had prayed to God to favour him with this blessing :

'O God, I am very short-tempered; Make me humble and calm.'

Hazrat Umar who became the second Khalifa of Islamic empire was a strong opponent of Mohamed Saheb in early days. But when he convinced himself of Mohamed Saheb's truthfulness, he at once accepted Islam. That year was 615 A.D. Thereafter he became faithful companion of Mohamed Saheb throughout life. Even Mohamed Saheb's marriage with his own daughter Hazrat Hafiza had taken place because of his own insistence:

The period of reign of Hazrat Umar as Khalifa for ten and a half years (634-644 A.D.) is known for a number of achievements, like excellent commander-in-chief, best ruler and as a just Khalifa, he had obtained people's love.

In order to know people's condition, every night Hazrat Umar came out silently. One night when he came out to know people's condition, a beautiful woman was singing a song in a sad tone standing in the balcony of her house :

'The night is dark and long,

But my husband is not with me,

My heart rends with the pain of separation.'

On hearing that woman's heart-rending song, Hazrat Umar became sad. After returning, he made inquiry about, who her husband was and where he was. It was learnt that the husband of that woman was in the army, and is at the war front only for about the last one year. On the very next day Hazrat passed the law :

"Even the smallest soldier should not be kept away on the front from his house for more than four years."

Hazrat Umar was also a Muslim following code of conduct. He did not get time during the day from the work of state administration. He therefore used to pray during the whole night. In the morning namaz (prayer), he used to recite long stanzas. He used to recite 'namaz' in the mosque always with the people of community, not as a single person.

He always used to say :

'To recite 'namaz' with community people is even more than doing worship for a number of nights'.

Some good sentences of Hazrat Umar have become proverbs today :

e.g. 'Do not leave today's work till tomorrow.'

'Keep fearing from something which you hate.'

'It is better to keep away from crime than to tolerate the trouble of forgivance.'

Hazrat Umar had understood the inner meaning of Islam. He had given the concrete form to the value-based, humanitarian approach of Islam in his own life.

'Don't look at anybody's 'namazas' and 'Rozas,' also look at his honesty and sincerity.'

Hazrat umar never felt ashamed of putting on patched clothes even after becoming a Khalifa. He was the first such Khalifa who had received the title of 'Amir-ul-Momin,' that is, the best commander-in-chief. The spread of Islamic empire had taken place during his reign. Credit to spread Islamic empire up to Mesopotamiya, Syria, Iran and Egypt goes to him. It was during his reign only that Islamic calendar had begun.

Besides the best ruler, and commander-in-chief, and pious Muslim, he was a just Khalifa too.

During the holy round of Kaba somebody put his foot through mistake on the 'chaddar' (a kind of sacred cloth) of Syria's famous chieftain jibilla. And he became highly angry. He strongly slapped the common man whose foot had been put upon the '*chaddar*'. In reply to it, that man did the same thing to jibilla. Now chieftain jibilla had been slapped. He therefore complained to Hazrat Umar. Hazrat Umar, after knowing the whole incident, said:

"The reply of your slap has been given to you through a slap'.

'But there must be punishment of death for a common man for his such misbehaviour with a high man like me.'

'It happened like that during the dark age (that is, the age of ignorance), not in Islamic rule. In Islam, everyone is equal.'

Hearing this, chieftain jibilla became angry and left.

During the war of Iraq, an Iranian soldier was brought to Madina as a prisoner-of-war. His name was Firoz. Once, one day when Khalifa Hazrat Umar was getting morning 'namaz' recited, Firoz gave six blows of dagger hidden by him on Hazrat Umar at a time. When the people around him tried to catch him he commited suicide with his own dagger. Hazar Umar was severely wounded by this attack. There was no hope of survival. Hazrat Umar then declared his final desire.

'If Hazrat Aisha (Mohamed Saheb's wife) gives consent, I should be buried near Hazrat Mohamed Saheb only'.

On 31 November, 644 A.D., Hazrat Umar breathed his last in Madina. According to his final desire he was buried near Mohamed Saheb only. Even today, he is taking rest in close proximity with Mohamed Saheb.

15.5 Khalifa Hazrat Usman

In 'Encyclopaedia Britanica' English spelling of Hazrat Usman's name, the third Khalifa of Islamic rule, has been made as 'Uthamn'. His original name, however, was Abu Umra. His father's name was Affan. At the fifth generation, the descendants of Usman were associated with the descendants of Hazrat Mohamed Paygambar. No clarification is available about the year of birth of Hazrat Usman, but he was six years younger than Hazrat Mohamed Paygambar. Such reference is found in Islamic history.

In that age of Arabia, Hazrat Usman was the man who accepted Islam for the first time among the rich and powerful families. Because of the acceptance of Islam his uncle Hakim tied his hands and legs, beat him severely and said: 'Give up Islam.'

In spite of suffering severe pain, Hazrat Usman spoke this much only: 'Uncle, I will not give up Islam even if you may kill me.' Because of jealousy, hatred and bad intention towards Mohamed Saheb, when Abu Lahab instigated his son Utba and made him give divorce to Rukaiya (Mohamed Saheb's divorced daughter), it was Hazrat Usman only who at once married to Rukaiya, and thus expressed his love towards Mohamed Saheb. Over and above this, when tyranny of opponents reached climax in Mecca, it was Hazrat Umar only who left Mecca with his wife Rukaiya.

After the death of second Khalifa Hazrat Umar, in 644 A.D. Hazrat Usman became the third Khalifa. The first six years of his rule as Khalifa (644-656 A.D.) passed very well. That period was the golden age of Hazrat Usman's reign. But thereafter problems began to arise and they began to worsen. Demand began to come forth to remove him from the rank of Khalifa: Rebels' anger towards him was on this point that he had given importance to nepotism in administration, although it was totally false. Hazrat Umar did not hesitate to remove even his own son-in-law from power. Hars Bin Haqm was the son of Hazrat Usman's uncle and son-in-law. He was appointed on an important post. But when Hazrat Usman felt that he did not discharge his duties honestly, he was at once removed from power, Hazrat Usman, then, had declared in public: 'The man who does not discharge his duties honestly is not fit to remain on any post.' In spite of such impartial attitude of Hazrat Usman, opposition against him went on expanding. He was threatened to give up the rank of Khalifa. Even at that time Hazrat Usman, with a calm voice, had said this much only :

> 'Allah has entrusted me with the responsibility of Khalifa. No threat shall stop me in maintaining my duty.'

Rebels got more excited seeing Hazrat Usman's such firmness. One day, with the intention of killing him, they entered his house forcibly. At that time Hazrat Usman was reading Quran-e-Sharif. For a moment, the rebels forgot to attack on Hazrat Usman who was reading Quran-e-Sharif, and said: 'How can one raise one's hand on such a servant of God?'

But the very next moment, without being led by emotional flow, a cruel rebel named Saudan gave a blow with his sword and killed him. On 18 Jilhaj, Hijari 35, 17 July, 656 A.D., after the Khilafat for 12 years, Hazrat Usman became the victim of rebels at the age of 82. The community, who received the title of 'Usmangani' by distributing all his wealth among the poor, who expanded the area of Kaba Sharif, who built Masjide Nabvi with strong foundation, and who spent life within the Allah-bound limits, the assassination of Hazrat Usman was momentary by untruth over truth. Such a victory may seem like being spread from the Cross of Jesus Christ to the bullet on Gandhi, but the truth does not lose the slightest shine.

5.6 Khalifa Hazrat Ali

Hazrat Ali Ibne Abi Talib Abdullahil Galib (R.A.)*, whose final resting place is in Najfe Asharaf of Iraq about thirty miles away from Karabala and for whom Hazrat Mohamed Paygambar had said :

'You only are my brother, religious authority and representative'.

That Hazrat Ali Ibne Abi Talib Abdullahil Galib also was one of the basic propagandists of Islam. After the wife of Mohamed Saheb, Hazrat Khadija, the first Arab to accept the preachings of Islam, was Hazrat Ali only. Hazrat Ali died on 21st Ramzan, Hijrat year 40 – 25th of January, 661 A.D. At the very time of doing Namaz, an enemy Ibne Muljin attacked on Hazrat Ali and that wound itself became the cause of his death. Another identity of Hazrat Ali can be given as the son-in-law of Mohamed Saheb, but Hazrat Ali himself was a learned and enlightened person. This can be seen on the basis of statements of his preaching. Let us ruminate his preachings worth incorporating in our life.

'When you happen to get worldly wealth and property, spend it all liberally for the needy, because wealth is transient and unsteady, which exists today and is lost the next day.

'Abundance of man's wealth conceals his faults. Even though he is a liar, every one believes true whatever he says.'

'Your handsomeness or beauty does not increase by the pomp of your clothes. But real beauty glitters by knowledge and high conduct.'

'Because of ignorance, high family and as its member becoming proud, O man, all the people have been born of the same parents.'

'You may become son of any person, but obtain high conduct.'

'If you desire that your friend may get tired of you, meet him daily, but if you aspire to make friendship stronger, meet him on alternate day.'

In Hazrat Ali's statements of preaching somewhere truthfulness, and somewhere the key of replenishing the path of life is also visible.

'Old age appears your head, but your head of greed and temptation does not over become old. Certainly, a greedy person in the world always remains in trouble.'

'Firmly hold the rein of your desires, and don't lose control in search of wages like an uncontrolled horse. In the name of Allah's oath, wages can't be obtained simply by desiring it.'

'Don't walk on this earth with false pride and stiffness, because the earth on which you walk with egoistic style, the dust of the same earth will spread over you in a short time'.

'Only the enlightened are the best because they can point the right path to those who seek guidance.'

'You aspire to remain immortal but the death continues to show edge of its sharp teeth, opening its wide mouth.'

'Let there be very short distance between your tomb and the person sleeping with you in the ashes of tomb, yet he is far away from you.'

'Never be in the company of ignorant people, rather, always remain afraid of them.'

'For every wound, one or some other remedy is available, but misconduct is such a thing that no remedy is available for it.'

Hazrat Mohamed called such an enlightened Hazrat Ali just before a few moments of his death. He offered a seat near him and then said :

'For the sake of God, give full consideration to the slave women and the rights of slaves. Give them food to their heart's content and good clothes to be put on. And always keep humble and lovable behaviour with them.'

Lots of salutation of all of us to such close companion of Mohamed Saheb and a great man of the age, Hazrat Ali.

PART–3

Selected Incidents Focussing on Non-Violence in the Lives of Hazrat Mohamed Paigmber and Saints of Islam

1

Hazrat Mohamed paygamber *(p.b.u.h.) sometimes used to take meat of a camel or a goat, but ordinarily his food contained date and water or loaf of barley and water only. He preferred milk and honey. But because they were costly, he did not take them more. Once a companion offered him olive flour and said:

'Rasullah, you must take such food only'.

Mohamed Saheb said, 'This food is of the spendthrift people', saying this he refused to take it. He had dislike for onion and garlic. He did not eat any food which contained onion and garlic. It was his order that no one should come for Allah's worship if he has eaten onion and garlic.

Hazrat Abu Aiyub +(R.A.) informs:

'One day we prepared food with onion and garlic and sent it to the holy paygambar, but he returned it without eating it. I was confused and at once reached him and asked:

'O Rasulallah, why did you send food back without eating it?'

The holy paygambar said,

'Food had smell of onion and garlic in it.'

Allah's messangers often visit me. I talk with them. They do not like the smell of onion and garlic. I therefore sent the food back, but you can eat it with pleasure.'

Hazrat Abu Aiyab heard the story of the holy paygamber and said,

'How can we prefer the thing which is not liked by the holy paygamber? After this incident, we too, gave up the use of onion and garlic in food.'

---

*(p.b.u.h.) - 'peace be upon him.'
+(R.A.) - *Rahemtullah Alayahi*

2

Once a poor, wretched person came to Mohamed Saheb ('Rasul-e-Pak') and said, 'O Rasulallah, I am hungry for a number of days, please give me something to eat.'

Mohamed Saheb asked in his home, 'Is there anything to eat?' 'There is nothing except water, came the reply.

He asked companions, 'Is there anyone who can make this poor man his guest?'

Hazrat Abu Talha stood up and said, 'O Rasulallah, I am making him my guest.'

And Hazrat Abu Talha reached his home, taking that poor man. He offered the seat to the guest, went inside and asked his wife, 'Is there anything to eat?'

The wife replied, 'Food is just enough for you only.'

After thinking for sometime, Abu Talha said, 'Extinguish all the lamps of the house.'

Then he called that poor man in the dark and served him food and he also sat with him. That poor man went on eating in the dark. Abu Talha continued to move his hand and mouth in such a way as if he also was taking food with that guest. After feeding the poor guest to his heart's content, he bade him good-bye. After the guest had left, the wife asked 'You fed the poor guest to his heart's content, and why did you pretend in the dark to be eating food?'

Hazrat Abu Talha said,

'You may experience shortage, but give as much as possible to the poor and the suppressed people.'

3

Quran-e-Sharif gives description of three types of neighbours: Such type of neighbours, that is neighbours who are good relatives also besides being good neighbours. Next, such neighbours as are not relatives, but are *just* neighbours. They include non-Muslims, too. Further such neighbours as may have come into contact by chance during travels, in offices or in any other way. With all these three types of neighbours, Islam orders to maintain good conduct and brotherly feeling. A man who keeps faith in Allah and the Day of Justice should not cause misery or give trouble to his neighbours. In one of the commandments, Mohamed Saheb ('Rasul-e-Pak') has said:

'He is not a Muslim who feeds himself to his heart's content, but keeps his nearby neighbours hungry.'

Once a follower requested Hazrat Mohamed paygamber:

'Your Honour, that woman is very much '*Namazi*' (a person who observes day-fasting) keeps, (*i.e.* observes) many day-fastings (rozas) donates a lot but harasses her neighbours by her bitter tongue :'

Hazur said: 'That woman shall go to hell, because she is not real Muslim whose mischiefs may be harassing her neighbour.'

4

Hazrat Mohamed hated divorce because God ('Khudatallah') also has hated divorce. To divorce a woman without any reason is a big crime in Islam, and a divorcer is an offender before God. Zenab was the daughter of Mohamed Saheb's ('Rasul-e-Pak') aunt's daughter. Zenab's father Jahash belonged to Dudan lineage of Kureshis. Mohamed Saheb advised the leaders of Dudan lineage to marry Zenab to Zeb. Zeb was a slave set free by Mohamed Saheb the suggestion of Mohamed Saheb, Zenab was married to Zeb.

Zenab had vanity of her dynasty and family. She behaved with her husband Zeb as if she had highly obliged that slave by marrying herself who was the daughter of a fair skinned Arab to a slave. Sometimes quarrels started between them because of Zenab's vainglorious nature. Being tired, Zeb thought of divorcing Zenab, and he went to Mohamed Saheb to ask for his permission. Mohamed Saheb asked Zeb,

'Why? Did you find any big fault in Zenab?'

Zeb replied, 'No, there is no big fault as such, but she is vainglorious. I cannot, therefore, live with her.'

'Go back, keep your wife with you only, and fear God.'

5

Hazrat Mohamed paygamber had spread his kingdom in the north from Syrian border to the Indian Ocean in south. In order to establish administration in different provinces of this vast state, the appointment of governors was made by 'Rasul-e-Pak (*i.e.* Hazrat Mohamed himself) whether the governor is capable enough to run the popular rule keeping faith in the principles of Islam or not was tested by Mohamed Saheb himself. Jabal's son Muaz was to be sent as the governor of Egypt ('Yemen'). Mohamed Saheb called Muaz and asked, 'In the administration of your province which thing will you believe authoritative to take decision?'

Muaz said, 'I will do it on the basis of commandments of Quran-e-Sherif.'

(Muaz said, 'I will do it on the basis of commandments of Quran-e-Sherif.)

Mohamed Saheb asked 'But if a commandment conforming to an occasion is not available in Quran, what will you do?'

Muaz said, 'At that time I will behave keeping paygamber's example before me.'

'But even conforming commandment may not be available in paygamber's example, what will you do?'

Muaz said, 'At that time I will take decision morally with my intelligence and cleverness.'

On hearing Muaz's reply Mohamed paygamber was pleased and preaching him said, 'Never give a judgement without listening well to the story of both the persons when they come to you for getting justice.'

6

Hazrat Mohamed paygamber was highly persistent about justice. Once a woman of Mukhzum family commited theft. A complainant came to Mohamed Saheb for justice. Mohamed Saheb had a great respect for Ousama Binzaidi. So the accused woman came to Mohamed Saheb with Ousama Binzaidi. On seeing Ousama Binzaidi, Mohamed Saheb spoke at once:

'Ousama, have you come to interfere with justice?'

On hearing Mohamed Saheb's question, Ousama's eyes bent down with shame.

Addressing the companions, Mohamed Saheb said:

The populace before you has been wiped out from over the earth because they did not do justice to the poor and the suffering people. I swear in God's name, if Fatima (Mohamed Saheb's dear daughter) has commited an offence, I will punish her even.'

7

Hazrat Mohamed paygamber, as far as possible, was not in favour of killing human beings and massacre in war. He had conquered Mecca with love and friendliness. At that time he possessed the equipped with arms. Army of ten thousand soldiers. Hazrat Umar had become the guide of this army.

In spite of this, Mohamed Saheb had given strict instruction to each and every sepoy that no one should use weapons. If an enemy opposes he should be arrested, but he should not be attacked.

At the time of Mecca's victory Hazrat Mohamed paygamber's army was lying out in a camp outside Mecca. On that day sentries on duty saw two persons making suspectable movement near the camp outside. They arrested him and brought them before Mohammed Saheb. Between these two persons one was Kureshi Sardar Abu Sufia, the die-hard enemy of Islam. He only had occupied Mecca. It was he only who had once planned a conspiracy to murder Mohamed Saheb, but he did not succeed in it. In spite of seeing such die-hard enemy before him in a mysterious condition, Mohamed Saheb did not even slightly go astray. He seated Abu Sufia with great respect near him and removing his fear, said :

'O Abu Sufia, due to your deeds, Muslims had to face a number of hardships for a long long period of 20 years. In spite of it, I forgive you.'

This created deep effect on the head and heart of Abu Sufia. He surrendered Mohamed Saheb because of this noble dealing and behaviour. And he accepted Mohamed Saheb as his commander and recognized Mecca's government as national government. Thus without droping a single drop of blood Mohamed Saheb secured victory over Mecca. His these thoughts were engraved on the hilt of Hazrat Mohamed paygamber's sword.

'Forgive the one who does injustice to you, unite with one who separates you from him, do good to one who practices evil with you, and always speak truth in spite of its going against you.'

8

Mohamed Saheb often used to receive gifts of gold, silver and precious things, but he did not keep those things even for a single night. As soon as the things were received he used to distribute them among the needy people. One night he felt somewhat uneasy. At last he asked Ayesha,

'Is there any gold or silver under our roof?'

Ayesha happened to remember, and she spoke out:

'Abba (Abu Bakr) has given some money for the poor, it is lying in the house.'

Mohamed Saheb said:

'Get that money distributed among the poor now only. You do not know that there should be no wealth under the roof of Saints.

9

The date was 17th of 'Ramzan', Hijri 2. The first collision between Kufre and Islam was to take place on the plains of Bhadra. This was the battle between truth and untruth. This battle was between faith and atheism. At the break of dawn Mohamed Saheb gave a call for 'namaz',

'O servants of Allah, it is time for 'namaz'.

On hearing Mohamed Saheb's voice, after washing hands and feet for 'namaz', companions gathered at one place. Mohamed Saheb got every one morning prayer' 'namaz' recited, and gave a short discourse on crusade:

Remember, victory or defeat does not depend upon the strength of number, upon the pomp and glory, upon plenty of weapons and unlimited means and materials. The most patience, firmness and important thing for victory is the trust Allah.

10

Hazrat Mohamed paygamber was busy negotiating with his companions. He said:

"After death, Allah will ask, 'O humble servant, I was ill and you did not come to inquire after my health."

The humble servant will say:

'O my God, how can I come to inquire after your health? You are the master of the whole world.'

Allah will ask again:

'O humble servant, I asked for food from you, and you had not given it to me.'

The humble servant will say:

'O my God, you are the master of the whole world. How can I give food to you?'

Allah will ask again:

'O humble servant, I asked for water from you and you did not give it to me.'

The humble servant will say:

'O my God, How can I give water to you? You are the master of the whole world.'

'Did you not know that my one humble servant was sick? You did not go to inquire after his health. Did you not know that my one humble servant had asked for food to you? And you did not give it to him. Did you not know that if you gave food to him, you would see me with him? My one humble servant asked for water from you, and you did not give it to him. If you gave him water, you would see me with him.'

11

Hazrat Mohamed paygamber Saheb was reaching the age of 63. He was keeping sick. Because of fever he felt very weak. In spite of this, by taking support of his both cousins Ali and Fajal, he used to come to mosque regularly to meet his companions, and recite 'namaz'. On that day, too, after 'namaz' he said to his companions:

'My companions, if I have done any harm to any of you, I am present here to give its reply. If there is any dues of any of you, whatever I have today, all that is of yours.'

One companion reminded, 'I had given three *'dirhams'* to a poor man on your word.'

At the very moment, Mohamed Saheb gave away three 'dirhams', and said:

'For our credit-debit, it is good to feel ashamed in this world so that we may not have to suffer pain at God's abode.'

12

Hazrat Mohamed paygamber never used to put on silken clothe. He used to say:

'A religious man should never put on silken clothes.'

Coloured clothes he used to put on occasionally. But he liked white coarse cotton clothe more, and mostly put on similar clothe only. He used to put on unstitched clothe more. Ordinarily, he used to wrap one white 'chaddar' from upper part of the body till the legs below, and both its ends were tied on the shoulder behind the neck. Mostly he remained bare-headed and bare footed. At times he used to put on a loose half-sleeved shirt and tied a piece of cloth round his head. He has never put on pyjamas. He has never kept with him more than one metallic pot with him.

His behaviour with the young and the old remained the same. He had love for children particularly more. While walking on the road, it was his routine to keep standing and start playing, with children in gally. These were the characteristics of Mohamed Saheb's nature: To go to inquire after a sick person's health, to accompany up to a little distance with a funeral procession of any one-a Muslim or non-Muslim and accept with pleasure an invitation given by a smallest person or even a slave.

13

Those were the days of war. Youths in large number were joining the war. During those days some one said to Mohamed Saheb,

'O paygamber, I want to go to war for the sake of Allah.'

Mohamed Saheb asked him:

'Is your mother alive?'

That young man said: 'Yes'.

Mohamed Saheb asked again:

'Is there anybody else to take care of her?'

The youngman replied: 'No'.

Mohamed Saheb said: 'Then go back, serve your mother, because heaven lies at her feet only.'

14

During the journey, once Mohamed Saheb was going on foot. When it was time for taking food, the group halted at one place. Everyone distributed work for preparing food. Paygamber Saheb accepted the task of collecting firewood.

The companions said:

'You may not take such trouble, please.'

We will do that work.

Mohamed Saheb said :

'But I don't want to keep myself higher than you. God does not love a person who considers himself higher than his companions.'

15

Once Hazrat Imam Abu Hanifa *(R.A.) was discussing something with Hazrat Imam Jafar Sadiq. Hazrat Imam Jafar Sadiq asked him:

'What is the identity of an intelligent man?'

Imam Abu Hanifa replied:

---

*(R.A. – Rahemtullah Alayahi)

'Someone who can know the secret between goodness and evil'.

You said:

'Even an animal has such understanding.

They do not harm those who behave well with them.'

At last Abu Hanifa asked,

'Then, what is the identity of an intelligent man according to you?'

You said,

'The man who practices the best of the two goodnesses and follows the less of the two evils is an intelligent man.'

16

'Auliya' Hazrat Malik Bin Dinar rented a house. A Jew used to live nearby. With a view to harassing you he always used to throw filth and garbage at the place where you recited namaz, you being bound by religious code to recite namaz five times a day. In spite of this, without uttering a single word, you yourself did cleaning and recited up 'namaz'. Such sequence went on for a long time. At last the Jew was tired, and one day, he asked you,

'I throw filth and garbage every day at the place of your reciting namaz, yet you do not speak anything.'

You said,

'What is trouble in it? I complete reciting namaz cleaning the filth and garbage you throw.'

The Jew said

'In spite of my giving so much trouble, without becoming angry, why did you go on suffering'?

You said,

'Khudatallah (God) has said:

'Be patient, be tolerant. People who get control over anger by becoming tolerant, their offences are forgiven, and they earn piety. Anger is a sign of destruction. Tolerance is the ornament of Islam.'

And on the same day, that Jew accepted Islam and became a 'namazi', binding himself by the code of Islam.

17

Hazrat Aboolak Kattani* (R.A.) was a pious, bound by religious code, devotee of his age. He remained absorbed in God's worship all the twenty-four hours. He set off for the Haj pilgrimage at a very small age. On the way your mother appeared in your dream one night. You were startled and woke up. You had set off on Haj pilgrimage without informing your mother. You realized about it, and returned. On returning home you found your mother hungry and thirsty, waiting for you at the door. You bent your head at her feet and said,"

'You have not permitted me for Hajj. On realizing it, I have come back.'

Mother said:

'My son, my tongue permitted you, but my heart did not accept it. My heart was restless without you. So I thought 'Let me keep standing at the door' waiting for you till you return.'

Hearing this, you postponed the intention of Hajj, and served your mother as long as she kept alive. It was only after her death that you left for Hajj.

Once when you were reciting 'namaz', a thief pulled away 'chaddar' from over your shoulder and ran away. But while running away, his foot struck against a stone. He fell down on the ground, his hands became useless. That thief realized his mistake. Pressing 'chaddar' into his mouth, he came to you. You had finished 'namaz'. Begging your pardon, the thief said,

*R.A. = *Rahimtullah Alayahi.*

'When you were reciting namaz, I played the mischief of stealing your chaddar. God has already given me its punishment. You, too, may forgive me.'

You said,

'I know nothing when you took my chaddar and when you ran away. Then what to forgive? Still you realized your mistake. That itself is your punishment. Go away, Allah will do you good.'

And life entered in the lifeless, useless hands of the thief. People were always eager to know the secret of such an intense attachment. So at the last moment of your life, when one disciple asked you, you said.

'For forty years I have not given place in my heart to anyone else except God. It is the execution of the principles of Islam that has taken me to God.'

Saying this, you set off on the path of God.

18

Hazrat Bayzid Bustami had obtained God's favour by his unlimited devotional worship. Your scholarship is well-known in paygamber's commandments. Whatever you had acquired had been obtained by God's and mother's service. In Islam mother's status is next to God. Heaven lies at mother's feet – you always used to tell this story in your preachings because in life you had given extreme importance to mother's service.

Once your mother asked for water at about 12 o'clock at night. You at once got up and ran to fetch water to the kitchen. Unfortunately, there was no water in the water pitcher. So carrying the pitcher and penetrating darkness of the desert, you set out in search of water.

Having not got water, your mother again slept whereas you continued search of water for the whole night in desert.

At last you came across a stream of water, and you reached back home with water.

When you reached home your mother was in deep sleep. You did not consider it proper to awaken her. So with the glass full of water you kept standing by her bed. Your mother changed side at dawn at the time of namaz, and woke up. She sensed everything seeing you standing with a glass of water. With emotional tenderness, she said,

'My son, why did you keep standing like this for the whole night with a glass of water?'

You said,

'Mother, I failed to give you water once. So I have stood like this so that you may not go to sleep again even, demanding painfully for water.'

Saying this, you offered a glass of water to mother. With your such service, your mother's eyes overflew with tears of joy and her heart was filled up with blessings.

19

There are two kinds of charities in Islam–'Zakat' and 'Kherat'. The former is a compulsory charity. Every Muslim has to set apart fortieth share of his movable and immovable property compulsorily every year as a charity. This duty is 'Zakat'. The other kind of charity in Islam is 'Kherat'. 'Kherat' is a voluntary charity. It is not compulsory. Word 'Kherat' has come down from the word 'Khairat'. 'Kher' means good, auspicious. That means every good act is a charity. ('Kherat') 'Zakat' can be exercised by only that Muslim who possesses movable – immovable property' whereas 'Kherat' can be exercised by every poor, rich, small or big Muslim. 'Kherat' can be offered in kind or cash. But 'Kherat' in the form of good deeds is even more important than that. Acts of small services like pointing the right path to someone who has lost the way, feeding the hungry, conveying the medicine to a patient in time or nursing him/her, helping a student in studies, making an illiterate person literate, helping a blind or an invalid person cross the road, - all these are the best forms of 'Kherat'.

When someone known to us dies, people mostly ask: how much property has he/she left behind? But after death when an angel will come to the tomb to carry him/her, he will ask the dead man,

'How much 'Kherat' (charity) have you exercised?'

At that time, good acts we did will be counted, and their value will be estimated.

Once a 'Sahabi' asked Hazrat Mohamed paygamber,

'My mother has expired, What should I do after her?'

Thinking about unbearable heat of the desert, Mohamed Saheb said,

'Get a well dug in your mother's name and quench the thirst of those who are thirsty.'

Awing says, more and more important but less and less given 'Kherat' is that of speech. Hazrat Mohamed Saheb specially recommended it. Basra's resident Abuzariya once requested paygamber Saheb to say something about manners. You said,

'Never say bad for any one at any time.'

If we shall implement such noble principles of 'Kherat' (charity) in practice, the world will overflow with love.'

20

In Islam, 'sabra', that is tolerance has been given special importance. That's why most of the Islamic saints had developed that virtue, believing it to be the path of devotional worship Noble example can be found in the life of Hazrat Usman Hayari, *(R.A.), too.

Once a Jew pressingly invited Hazrat Usman Hayari for a dinner. You reached his home in time. That Jew had invited

---

*(R.A. Rahemtullah Alayahi)

you just to insult you. So as you entered his house, he shouted, 'Get out, a hungry wolf !'

So saying, that Jew drove you out. You returned. You might have walked a little distance, that Jew at once called you back.

You came back, then again he abused you and drove you out. Without uttering a single word, you returned. That Jew called you back the third time and insulted you, saying,

'Take this stone, and eat it.' You returned.

In spite of being insulted three times, you did not utter a single word. Seeing your tolerance, that Jew was surprised, and calling you for the fourth time, he asked,

'In spite of being insulted so many times, why don't you become angry?'

With a smiling face, you said,

'God intensely loves a person who keeps patience. Besides, the tolerance lying in me is not more than even of an ant. I have not cultivated tolerance to the extent of an ant which it has to exercise to procure a grain of corn. I pray to cultivate tolerance even more than this which may be befitting to a man.'

Having been wonderstruck, that Jew fell at your knee.

Once you were passing through a road. Your disciples were with you. Suddenly, someone from above poured a bucketful of ashes on you. Your whole body and head was filled with ashes. One of your disciples became angry and began to quarrel with the person who threw ashes. You called the disciple back and said,

'The head which deserves the infernal fire has been covered with ashes by him. I am, therefore, grateful to him.'

So saying you continued walking.

21

'Hazrat Ahmed Rave's devotional worship went on for all the twenty-four hours. He did not sleep even at night, yet there were no signs of sleep in his eyes. Light always splashed out in his eyes. Once a person asked him.

'You do worship by keeping awake for a number of nights. Why don't you take a little rest?'

You explained,

'God has made heaven and hell both. I am the servant nearer to God, yet I do not know what will be my end? Then how can I sleep?'

One disciple came near you and bending his head, said,

'In the market one person has been doing a lot of wickedness to you.'

You said,

'Go back, bring him with honour before me and make him wealthy, by giving whatever he wants.

That disciple continued to see with surprise. Explaining to him, you said, 'The man who slanders me and practices wickedness with me makes me intensely pious. So should I not give him something in return for piety I received through him?'

22

Hazrat Rafi Balvi and Hazrat Ibrahim Bin Adham were well-known for God's worship and controlled, pious life. Once both the devotees accidentally met in a mosque of Mecca. It was a meeting between the two after a long long time. So after reciting 'namaz' both of them kept absorbingly busy talking in a corner. The discussion of God's worship and pious life started.

Hazrat Rafiq Balvi said,

worn out with the beating of hand-blows and kicks and a thick whip. Still at every blow, utterances like 'Ya Allah' used to come out of his mouth. Hazrat Abu Hasan Noori happened to pass thereby. This scene struck his eyes. For a few moments he continued to see this scene. Seeing God's light on the old man's face and hearing Allah's name in his mouth, he (*i.e.* Hazrat Abu Hasan Noori) knew that this man is God's pious servant. Stopping the policemen piling up mountain of pains on that old man's body, he asked that old man,

'In spite of this much old age, why is no effect of the beating, striking your body not seen on your face?'

That old man said, 'The relation of tolerance is with courage and fearlessness, not with physical strength and miracle'

Allah's devoted worshipper asked to understand the spell of this common man,

'What is the meaning of patience'?

That old man replied, 'Bear hardships with that much pleasure as much you experience at the time of your release from hardships.'

A man was often turning his hand round his beard. Somebody complained to you about it. You called that man and said,

'At the time of reciting 'namaz' keep your hand away from God's beard and be absorbed in God.'

And this story spread widely that you recognized an ordinary man's beard as God's beard. This story reached Khalifa's ears, and so Khalifa imprisoned you and asked an explanation.

'Why did you say an ordinary man's beard as God's beard?'

You said,

'This world is God's creation. Every human being has been created by God. Then how can a man's beard be man's own?'

And Khalifa apologized and set him free.

25

The philosophy of Islam chiefly depends on the principles of God's worship and human values. To be one with Gods' worship, Islam has accepted duties like 'namaz', 'roza', 'zakat', and Hajj. These duties help every Muslim to take him near God. Of course, among these duties, three duties, that is, 'namaz', 'roza' and Zekat are compulsory, whereas in Hajj, a little concession is given.

Hajj means religious pilgrimage, it means going round Baytulla's holy place. There is a statement in Quran-e-Sharif about Hajj: A person who is strong and capable enough for Hajj's travel, Hajj is a duty for him. Thus for a poor, helpless and incapable Muslim, there is concession about Hajj's duty. Who can be considered eligible for Hajj? A Muslim who has discharged all his responsibilities, and has provided enough for the maintenance of his family is considered eligible for Hajj. Such a person, even though he is happy and well-provided, is considered an offender if he does not perform Hajj. There are several illustrations available from Islam by which a Muslim has earned the reward of piety of his home by sincerely discharging three duties – 'namaz', 'roza' and Zekat – of Islam and by sincerely implementing humanitarian principles of Islam. Hazrat Abdullah Bin Mubarak was taking rest in Baytullah after Hajj, and he went to sleep. In his dream, he heard two angels talking.

One said, 'How many people came to Hajj this time'?

The other replied, 'About one lakh people performed Hajj this time.'

The first one asked, 'From among one lakh Hajis whose Hajj has been accepted by God'?

The other said, 'No one's. This time God has accepted Hajj of a shoemaker of Damisk who has not even turned up for Hajj!'

And Hazrat Abdullah Bin Mubarak's* eyes opened. Owing to eagerness of making self-inquiry about the fact seen and heard in the dream, he reached Damisk. Searching continuously, he reached the shoemaker's place at Damisk. After blessing, he asked, 'This year from among one lakh persons who came to perform Hajj, God has accepted no one's Hajj, but God has conferred the piety of performing Hajj in Damisk to you at your home! What kind of worship did you make that God bestowed the piety of Hajj even without performing it?'

The poor shoemaker was a little perplexed at first, and surprised. After some time, on becoming comfortable, he said,

'With the strong desire of performing Hajj, I had saved and credited some money earned from my butcher's income. But just before a few days, I came to know the condition of my neighbour. His stove did not light continuously for seven days. His children strove vainly with hunger. My heart intensely lamented, knowing it. And I gave away to him the money I had credited for Hajj.'

Realizing the real significance of Hajj, you said,

'To give food to the hungry and wish well of every one, known is as much important as Hajj's piety.'

Saying this, and saluting that poor Muslim's real worship, you took leave.

26

It was time of war. Hazrat Abdullah Bin Mubarak* was fighting on the battlefield, and there was a shouting call for 'namaz', You put the sword into the scabbard, cleaned your

---

*(R.A. – Rahemtullah Alayahi)

hands and feet, and completed 'namaz'! After completing it, the Jew fighting against you in war also started his prayer. When the Jew was doing prayer, a thought flashed into your head.

'How, if I kill this praying Jew at this very moment by giving a blow?'

And you took the sword out from the scabbard. Your steps started toward the Jew. You had hardly walked a few steps when the voice arose from your heart:

> 'A Muslim who gives a blow to an enemy engrossed in prayer is punished on the Day of Judgement. So stop.'

You stopped. Having realized that your steps went against the principles of Islam, you began to cry. Seeing you profusely dropping tears, that Jew came near you, and making you peaceful, asked the reason of crying. You said, 'I am guilty of God and of you. An inhuman thought came to my mind to kill you at the time when you were praying. But my God has saved me of that one offence. Pardon me and my guilt for my such offence. Otherwise, I will have to endure its punishment on the Day of Judgement.'

That Jew was awestruck on hearing this. The sword which he had lifted to deroot the principle of Islam, the same principles had given him life. At that very moment he threw away the sword, and accepted Islam.

Hazrat Sahal Tastarin had imbibed religious-mindedness through his father Abdulla. By cultivating control over mind, it was Hazrat Sahal's distinct style to keep engrossed continuously in God's worship. He constantly tried techniques to have control over his mind. Once he was performing journey. There itself his unsteady mind had a desire to eat bread and fish. You tried very hard to withdraw your mind from it, but the mind was not ready to be withdrawn. At last you did a trick. Reaching the market of Kufa town, you stopped a camel-cart driver and asked,

'How much hiring charge do you get per day if you give the camel-cart on hire?'

The camel-cart driver said,

'Two diharam'.

You said,

'You release the camel and harness me in its place. I will pull your camel-cart for the whole day. Please allow me the time for reciting 'namaz' at its time.

What remuneration will you give me, if I pull your cast for the whole day?'

Hearing this, the camel-cart driver was surprised, yet he said,

'I will give you one 'diharam'.

And Hazrat Sahal Tastarin pulled the camel-cart for the whole day. That camel-cart driver gave him one 'diharam'.

At that time the whole body was drenched with sweat and had been tired. You bought bread and fish with the help of that one 'diharam' and addressing your mind, said with the tired body.

'Take this bread, eat fish, but remember this much: When you have desire to eat such delicious food, you will have to perspire by becoming a beast. Controlling thus his unsteady mind, Hazrat Sahal was once sitting in his hut.

A disciple entered inside. Sitting calmly in the midst of a group of snakes, you were worshipping God. Frightened on seeing this, that follower instantly ran out, and by keeping himself outside, he asked,

'May I come in?'

'But inside, there is a group of snakes around you. I feel frightened.'

You said,

'As long as we shall continue to fear of any animal, we will not be able to conquer any step of progress. We will have to accept the principle of co-existence through love.'

27

It is at present that talk about protection of values in education goes on, but the worshippers of Islam have shown it practised in their lives. Hazrat Madni was very learned. Being impressed with his knowledge, a number of wealthy persons had proposed to convey his maintenance at his door, yet Hazrat Madni earned his living by teaching them in school. As a teacher, he had accepted several principles. One of them was: 'Take salary only for the days on which you teach.'

Once Hazrat Madni became ill. He could not attend school for a month. The administrators of school sent remuneration at his house, considering his one month's sick leave. Returning that remuneration Hazrat Madni informed,

'How can I take remuneration for the days on which I have not given training'?

In spite of weak economic condition of the house, Hazrat Madni could not get up from the bed and after his death, with the intention of giving his salary to his wife, the administrator of the school himself went to his house, and keeping in mind the condition of the house, he requested his wife to accept the salary. The wife who has digested her husband's principles in life humbly refused to accept money and said,

'Many many thanks to you.

But I cannot take the salary which my husband did not take while he was alive, after his death.'

With the commercial ideas pushed into the field of education today, Hazrat Madni's ideas would certainly cause surprize, but no support is required to say that they are true.

28

Once a Jew's coffin passed by the side where Mohamed Saheb was sitting. Mohamed Saheb stood up, and respected the coffin. Seeing this, a man asked you,

'Paygamber Saheb, this coffin belongs to a Jew (non-Muslim). What is the necessity of respecting it so much?'

You said,

'Does a Jew have no embodied soul'?

(Bukhari – Muslim).

Once a follower said to you requestingly,

'You pray to God against those who believe in other deities, and give them a curse.'

Mohamed Saheb said quietly,

'God has sent me doing kindness and kindness only, not to give a curse.'

(Muslim).

29

A follower came to Mohamed Saheb.

There was something wrapped in a piece of cloth with him. Giving it to Mohamed Saheb, he said,

'O paygamber, when I was coming through the forest, I heard the voice of young ones of a bird. I caught them throwing a blanket over them. Mother of young ones began to make sounds like 'chi, chi'. On seeing this I caught her, too.

Youngones and their mother are in this cloth. I give it to you as a present.

Please oblige me by accepting it.'

Mohamed Saheb continued to see the young ones and their mother shivering with terror. Then with some dislike on the face, said,

'Go, leave the youngones and their mother back to the place where you had caught them from, now and now only.'

(Abu Daud).

30

Once a follower stole and brought some eggs from the nest of a bird. Mohamed sahib came to know about it. He asked that follower,

'Go, leave the eggs back into the nest.'

31

Once a Jewish woman, in order to kill Mohamed Saheb, gave him food, dropping poison into it. Having doubt, Mohamed Saheb inquired about it. At last that Jewish woman confessed,

'Yes, I have dropped poison into Mohamed Saheb's food.'

Having heard this, companions and followers got excited. Every one became eager to kill that woman. But Mohamed Saheb made everyone calm, and without uttering a single word of anger, pardoned that woman.

'Forgivance is an ornament of a hero' is not the ornament of Hinduism alone, but forgivance and patience lie within the root of the principles of Islam, too. There is no place for violence and inhumanity in it at all. Mohamed Saheb had to suffer a number of insults and pains in spreading and propagating Islam, yet sense of taking revenge never entered in his life–story.

Once someone asked Mohamed Saheb,

'Who can be considered strong?'

You said,

'Really strong is not someone who suppresses others with

his muscle power, but really strong is he who suppressed anger with his willpower.'

32

Sufi saints of Islam had also incarnated the subtle concept of non-violence in their thoughts and behaviour.

Baba Farid was the disciple of Sufi saint Kutbuddin Bakhtiyar Kaki. According to the preceptor's command, Baba Farid performed very hard worship. He lived in the forest and suffered hardships. He worshipped God by eating leaves of trees in the forest. Thus after performing worship for a number of years, he went to meet his mother. His hair and beard had profusely grown. Long hair of the head was entangled.

He had put on only minimum clothes as were just enough to cover his body.

Mother was pained to see the condition of her son. She seated her son by her side. She took her son's head in her lap and rolled her hand in entangled hair.

At that time Baba Farid said,

'Mother, please do not roll your hand in my hair. The entangled hair gets pulled. Therefore I feel pain.'

Mother heard son's narrative. Then she said,

'My son, you feel pain while rolling hand in your hair, then how much pain would have those trees experienced whose leaves you plucked and ate?'

And Baba Farid was enlightened.

He said in his preaching,

'Absorb yourself in God's worship in such a way that no one else, except you, should suffer pain.'

Conclusion

While summarizing the study of Islam and Non-violence, it is befitting to cite many ideas of Gandhiji on Islamic ideology.

- "I think, Islam is also a peace-loving religion such as Christianity, Buddhism and Hinduism. No doubt, there is difference in standards. But every religion aims at peace."[1]
- "God is One. A Muslim is a brother of another Muslim. All Muslims practice these principles of Islam. These principles are unique parts, which are imparted into Indian Culture. These two are Islamic Contributions. The concept of unity, 'man is brother of man' is accepted by Hindu philosophers at higher level of philosophy. Even though Hindu theology ascertains the Oneness of God, the followers of Hinduism are not as strict as the believers of Islam in accepting this truth. One cannot deny this fact."[2]
- "For converting into Islam, Holy Quran never tells to use the force. Thus, the Holy Book says 'No compulsion in religion.' The whole life of Mohammad, the Messenger of Allah nullifies the idea of compulsion and coercion in religion. I am not aware of any Muslim who supported compulsion in religion. If the compulsion is to be used for conversion into Islam, then the Universal Religion would come to cease."[3]
- "I am of the opinion that the believers of Islam use sword time and again. But, it is not due to the teachings of Holy Quran. I opine that they are thankful to the circumstances in which the Islam was born."[4]

- "I have read Holy Quran again and again. It not only encourages adopting whatever is good in my religion as well as in the religions of the world, but also makes me do so as my duty."[5]
- "I surely believe that Islam is a God-created religion. So, I believe, Holy Quran is also created by God. I believe, Mohammad Saheb is Messenger of God."[6]
- "My conclusive opinion is that basically, Holy Quran commends the non-violence. It says, non-violence is better than violence. It ordains to follow nonviolence as a sense of duty. Violence is permissible only under certain needs."[7]
- "Even the meaning of Islam is Peace, that is, non-violence. Badshah Khan is a strict Muslim. He never neglects Prayer and Fasting. He has accepted non-violence as a religious duty. If a person alleges that he cannot strictly practice the religion, then there is no solution for his problem. I, myself, cannot follow my religion as such. I have to accept this truth with humility. If anything is left out in my practice, it is the standard, not the article. But, if any body doubts the presence of non-violence preaching in Holy Quran, then the doubt is spurious. There is no need to discuss it."[8]

References

1. Nav Jivan - 23rd January 1927, p. 164.
2. Gandhjino Akshar Deh - Part 40, p. 57.
3. Agen - Part 21, pp. 195-196.
4. Nav Jivan - 23rd January, 1927, p. 164.
5. Harijan Bandhu - 29th October, 1939, p. 272.
6. Harijan Bandhu - 14th July, 1940, p. 143.
7. Agen, p. 142.
8. Harijan Bandhu—October, 1939, p. 246.

Glossary

1. **Abdullah bin Amar** — Abdullah bin Amar bin Al-A'as accepted Islam before his illustrious father. He belonged to the tribe of Salim, a branch of the Quraish. He used to write down traditions spoken by the Prophet Mohammad (Sal-allahu-aleihi-wasallam). He was so devout, pious and God-fearing that he lost his eyesight owing to excessive weeping. It is said that he died either in 63 or 73 A.H. at Makkah.

2. **Abdullah Ibn Mas'ud** — Abdullah Ibn Mas'ud's real name was Abdullah and his father's name was Mas'ud. Abdullah Ibn Mas'ud, at the beginning of his youth, used to tending the flocks of a Quraish chieftain, Uqbah ibn Muayt. People called him "Ibn Umm Abd," the son of the mother of a slave. Very soon, Abdullah ibn Mas'ud became a Muslim. Abdullah ibn Mas'ud gave up tending sheep in exchange for looking after the needs of the blessed Prophet. Abdullah ibn Mas'ud received a unique training in the household of the Prophet. He was under the guidance of the Prophet, he adopted his manner and followed his every trait until it was said of him, "He was the closest to the Prophet in character." He was present at the Battle of Badr. When

he died at Madina in year 32 A.H., he was 60 years old.

3. Abu Ayub Ansari

Abu Ayub Ansari's full name is Khalid bin Zaid Ansari Khajrazi, but he is well known by his surname. After his flight to Medina, the Holy Prophet (Sal-allahu-aleihi-wasallam) fixed his residence at Abu Ayyub's house. Abu Ayub Ansari accepted his hospitality. This honour was not shared by anyone else. He joined the Prophet (Sal-allahu-aleihi-wasallam) in all his fights and also took part in the great expedition sent by Hazrat Muawiyah against Constantinople. He died in 51 A.H. at Constantinople and, according to his last wish; he was buried at the foot of the wall of the city. He narrated many traditions from the Holy Prophet Mohammad (Sal-allahu-aleihi-wasallam).

4. Abu Bakr Siddique

Abu Bakr Siddique's full name is Abdullah bin Osman Abu Qahafah. He was the first and the foremost companion of the Holy Prophet (Sal-allahu-aleihi-wasallam) in all his dangers and difficulties and was the first leader of the believers after the Prophet's (Sal-allahu-aleihi-wasallam) passed and the first male who accepted Islam when the new faith was announced. He was born at Makkah, two years and a half before the invasion of Makkah by Abraha, the ruler of Yemen and he died at Medina at the age of 60 years after a rule of 2 years and 5 months. The Holy Prophet (Sal-allahu-aleihi-wasallam) gave him the title of 'Siddique' (Extremely truthful) and praised him in many terms.

5. Abu Dawood — His full name is Abu Da'ud Suleiman Ibn Ash'ath al-Azadi al-Sijistani. He was a noted collector of hadith i.e. the sayings and traditions of Prophet Muhammad, and wrote the third of the six canonical hadith collections recognized by Sunni Muslims, *Sunan Abi Da'ud*. He was born in Sijistan or Sagestan, in Afghanistan in 817, and died in 888. Widely travelled among scholars of ahadith, he went to Iraq, Egypt, Syria, Saudi Arabia, Khurasan, Nishapur, and Marv among other places in order to collect ahadith. He was primarily interested in law, and as a result, the collection by him focuses largely on legal ahadith. From about 50,000 ahadith, he chose 4,800 for inclusion in his work based on their superior authenticity. *Sunan Abi Da'ud*, containing some 4800 hadith, is his principal work, but he wrote some 21 books in all.

6. Abu Huraira — Abu Huraira's original name was Bad-Shams or Abd-Amer. Abu Huraira is also called so, for his love for a pet cat. After conversion to Islam, he changed his name to Abdullah or Abdur Rehman. He accepted Islam in the year of the Siege of Khaiber. He was greatly attached to the Prophet Mohammad (Sal-allahu-aleihi-wasallam). He had

Abu Talib ibn 'Abd al-Muttalib. His mother was Fatima bint Asad. He was raised in the household of Muhammad. Ali, along with some members of the Banu Hashim clan, was Hanifs prior to the coming of Islam. When Muhammad reported that he had received a divine revelation, Ali was about ten years old. Ali was the first male to enter Islam. At the age of 22 or 23, Ali migrated to Medina shortly after Prophet Muhammad did. For the ten years that Muhammad led the community in Medina, Ali was extremely active in his service, serving in his armies, the bearer of his banner in every battle, leading parties of warriors on raids, and carrying messages and orders. As one of Muhammad's lieutenants, and later his son-in-law, Ali was a person of authority and standing in the Muslim community. After the assassination of the third *Caliph*, Osman Ibn Affan, the Sahaba in Medina chose Ali to be the new Caliph. He was the *caliph* between 656 and 661 CE. He encountered defiance and civil war during his reign. While Ali was praying in the mosque of *Kufa*, a *Khawarij* assassinated him with a strike of a poison-coated sword. Ali died on the 21st of Ramadan in the city of Kufa on February 28, 661 CE. Muslims greatly respect Ali for his knowledge, belief, honesty, his unbending devotion to Islam, his deep loyalty to Muhammad, his equal treatment of all Muslims and his generosity in forgiving his defeated enemies.

11. Ayat — Verse or sentence in Quran. The meaning of Ayat is miraculous sign. There are Five methods of Ayat countings. The School of Kufa says they are 6239. The School of Basrah says they are 6204. The School of Sham says they are 6225. The School of Makkah says they are 6219 and the School of Madinah says they are 6211. The difference in the number of Ayats makes no difference in the meaning of Holy Quran.

12. Battle of Badr — The place of Badr is situated at 130 kilometres to southwest of Madina city, in Saudi Arabia. The city of Makkah at that time was one of the richest and most powerful pagan cities in Arabia, which fielded an army three times larger than that of the Muslims. The Battle of Badr was fought on March 17, 624 CE (17 Ramadan 2 AH in the Islamic calendar.) The Muslims and the pagans of Makkah had fought several smaller skirmishes in late 623 and early 624. The Battle of Badr however was the first large-scale engagement between the two forces. The battle was extremely significant. The Muslim victory also signalled other tribes that a new power had arisen in Arabia and strengthened Prophet's authority as leader of the often-fractious community in Medina. Local Arab tribes began to

convert to Islam and ally themselves with the Muslims of Medina.

13. Bukhari

Abu 'Abdullah Muhammad Ibn Isma'il al-Bukhari was born on the 13th of the Islamic month of Shawwal, 194 AH, in the famous city of Bukhara, - present day Uzbekistan - in Afghanistan. The father of Imam Bukhari, Isma'il Ibn Ibrahim Ibn Mughirah al-Ja'fi, was a great muhaddith and ascetic. From him Imam Bukhari inherited his characteristics of literary zeal and excellence. During his infancy, his father passed away. His mother took up the entire responsibility of bringing him up. Imam Bukhari became blind at a young age. It was said, by the Grace of God, later he regained his eyesight. At the age of eighteen, he visited Makkah accompanied by his mother and elder brother, Ahmad ibn Isma'il. After performing the pilgrimage, his brother returned with the company of his mother, but Imam Bukhari stayed there for further education. He was full of intelligence and excellent memory. Imam Bukhari travelled to cities everywhere for the transmission of Ahadith. He had gained immense knowledge. Even though he was rich by birth, Imam Bukhari was a simple and hard working person. He would fulfill his own needs by himself. Despite having a lot of wealth and status, he always kept the minimum number of servants required and never indulged himself in this matter.

14. Ibn Wahb — Ibn Wahb's full name is Abu Muhammad Abd Allah Ibn Wahb Ibn Muslim. He was born at Old Cairo in Zu'l Kaada in the year 125 A.H. He was a member, by adoption, of the tribe of Quraish, a doctor of the sect or Malik: a native of Egypt was a mawla to Rehana, who was herself a mawla to Abu Abd arRahman Yazid Ibn Unais, of the tribe of Fihr. He was one of the great Imams of that age. He was a disciple of Imam Malik Ibn Anas. Ibn Wahb left his native town to meet Imam Malik in the year 148 A.H. He stayed with Imam Malik till the death of Imam Malik. Imam Malik conferred him with honours like 'Imam' and 'Mufti'. For Twenty years he worked hard to edit the works of his master, Imam Malik Ibn Anas, and to compile them into a Book, namely Al Muwatta. Ibn Wahb died in Old Cairo on Sunday, on 24th of Shaaban in the year 197 A.H.

15. Jabir Bin Abdullah — His full name was Jabir ibn Abdullah ibn Amr ibn Haram *Al-Ansari*. He was born in Yathrib 15 years before the Hijra. He belonged to a poor family of Yathrub. He was from the tribe of Khizraj. His mother was Naseeba binte Uqba ibn Uddi. He accepted Islam when he was a young boy. He is known to have fought in 19 battles, including Badr, under the command of Prophet Muhammad. He was a trusted Sahaba. He was present during the conquest of Makkah.

He fought in the battles of Basra, Siffin, and Nahrawan under the command of Ali ibn Abi Talib. Due to old age, Jabir was unable to participate in the Battle of Karbala. Jabir had a long life and became blind in his old age. He was poisoned by Al-Hajjaj bin Yousuf Thaqfi the age of 94 years because of his loyalty to *Ahl al-Bayt*. He was buried in Madain near *Baghdad* at the bank of river *Tigris*. His died in 78 AH (697).

16. Khadijah

Khadijah Bint Khuwaylid was the First wife of Prophet Muhammad. She was the wealthiest person in Makkah. She always thought about helping the poor and sharing their sorrow and difficulties, and solving their problems. Therefore, they called her "Ummul Yatama," meaning, "Mother of the Orphans". She married twice. Twice she became widow. The third time, at the age of 40, she married young Muhammad, who was 25 years old. She was the first wife of Prophet Muhammad. She was the first woman to accept the religion of Islam. Prophet Muhammad never intended to marry another woman while Hazrath Khadija was alive. Their married happy life continued, during which she gave birth to Al-Qasim and Abdullah or Al-Tayib. She also gave birth to four daughters namely, Zainab, Ruqaiyah, Fatimah, and Umm Kulsum. Prophet Muhammad loved her and respected her very much. She was one of the four virtuous women of the world, namely Asiyah wife of Pharoah, Mariam, mother of Jesus, Khadija bint Khuwalaylid and Fatima bint Muhammad.

17. Mohammad

Mohammad Bin Abdullah was born in Makkah around 570 CE into the Banu Hashim clan of the Quraish tribe. His father was Abdullah and his mother was Amina. When he was about forty years old, he is said to have experienced a divine revelation while he was meditating in a cave outside Makkah. He began to preach to his kinfolk first privately and then publicly. As a result, the pagans threatened prophet Muhammad and his followers. During this period, Muhammad was protected by his uncle *Abu Talib*. When he died in 619, the leadership of the Banu Hashim passed to one of Muhammad's enemies, 'Amr ibn Hisham, who withdrew the protection and stepped up persecution of the Muslim community. In 622, Muhammad and many of his followers fled to the neighboring city of Yathrib or Medina. This migration is called the Hijra.

18. Muslim

Imam Muslim's full name is Abu Al Hussain Muslim, Ibn Al Hajjaj Al Qushairi. He was born at Naishapur, in the year 204 A.H. He collected many authentic traditions of Prophet. His book is called Sahihu Muslim. His book is

married to Prophet Muhammad. When Umar was a child, he used to graze the flocks of goats and sheep of his maternal aunts. Among the Quraish of Makkah, only seventeen persons could read and write, and Umar was one of them. Umar was a skillful rider. He was very intelligent and shrewd. He was a good public speaker. On several occasions, he successfully undertook ambassadorial missions on behalf of the Quraish. He was always prepared to stand up against the oppressor and espouse the cause of the weak. He was a successful trader and he undertook journeys to Syria, Iraq, Yemen, and elsewhere. When Umar migrated from Makkah, he was one of the richest Quraish merchants. Umar had three wives. His first wife was Qariba bint Abi Umayya al-Makhzumi. She belonged to the same clan as the mother of Umar. His second wife was Zainab bint Maziun. She was the sister of Usman bint Maz'un, an early companion, for whom the Holy Prophet had great regard. She was the mother of Abdullah and Hafsah. His third wife was Malaika bint Jarul al-Khuzai. She was also called Umm Kulsum. When the Holy Prophet (peace be on him) proclaimed his apostlehood, Umar, a young man of strong convictions, held the new faith to be a sacrilege of the idols of Katbah. He went to the Quraish and participated in their counsels. Then the meeting invited volunteers who would kill the Prophet. Umar volunteered to kill the Prophet. Meanwhile, he was compelled to go to the house of his sister, Fatima and Brother-in-Law Saeed Bin Zaid, who became Muslims. Sister Fatima made him read some Ayats of Quran. Umar felt that those verses of Ta Ha were addressed to him in person, and the mysterious Ta Ha referred to Umar-the Man. Then, he said to his sister, "I came to you as an enemy of Islam; I go from you as a friend of Islam. I had buckled this sword to slay the Prophet of Islam; I now go to him to offer him allegiance." Then Umar became a prominent follower of Islam. The Prophet took Umar's daughter Hafsah as his third wife. After many years, he became the Second Khalifa, after the death of Abu Bakr in the year 13 AH. For ten years, he ruled religiously. He was killed by Firoz, a Persian slave, in the year 23 AH. In his times, the Islamic empire spread a lot.

25. Yathrib/Madina — Yathrib is also known as Al-Madina, the City. Prophet Mohammad took shelter in Yathrib, after making Hizrath from Makkah. Gradually, the Yathrib became a 'Madinatun Nabi' or 'the City of Prophet'. It is situated within the area of Hijaz in Saudi Arabia. Prophet Mohammad was buried in Yathrib or in 'Madinatun Nabi'.

26. Zaid

Zaid: full name is Zaid Ibn Thabit. His mother was An-Nawar bint Malik. Zaid was 13 years old at the time of Battle of Badr. Prophet Muhammad did not allow him in war preparations. Zaid decided to learn the Qur'an, whatever part was revealed, by heart. He did so. Then, Prophet Mohammad asked Zaid to learn the Hebrew and Assyrian languages. Later on, he was appointed as scribe to handle correspondence and to collect and keep record of the Qur'anic verses. Zaid was not the only one who acted as a scribe for the Prophet. There were forty-eight persons, who used to write for Prophet. Zaid was very prominent among them. He used his time to recite the Qur'an, and continued to learn the Quranic verses as they were recited by Prophet Muhammad. Zaid later volunteered to fight when he was 19 years old. This time he was accepted in the ranks of the Muslim army. After the death of Prophet Muhammad, the task fell on Zaid to authenticate the first and most important reference for the Ummah of Muhammad. This became an urgent task, because many persons who memorised Quran died in the Battle of Yamamah. Umar Ibn al Khattab convinced the Khalifa Abu Bakr that the Quran should be collected in one manuscript. During Abu Bakr's reign as caliph, Zaid Ibn Thabit was given the task of collecting the

Quranic verses from all over Arabia. Zaid diligently started locating the Quranic material and collecting it from every authentic source. When Zaid had completed his task, he left the prepared documents with Abu Bakr. Before he died, Abu Bakr left the documents with Umar. Umar left it with his daughter Hafsah. Hafsah, Umm Salamah, and Ayeshah were wives of Prophet Muhammad, who memorized the Qur'an. During his caliphate, Osman obtained the manuscript of the Quran from *Hafsah*. He again summoned Zaid Ibn Thabit, and some other companions to make copies of Quran. Zaid was put in charge of the task. The style of Arabic dialect used was that of the Quraish tribe. Zaid and other companions copied many copies. One of these was sent to every Muslim province for reference. The wrong or doubtful copies were burnt down everywhere. The Caliph Osman kept a copy for himself and returned the original manuscript to *Hafsah*.

References

(1) "Islam Kya hai?" *(Earlier pages of the book are missing, so more details are not possible).*

(2) "Islam - suvarnayug", *Chunilal Purushotamdas Barot, Gujarat Vidyapith, Amdavad.*

(3) 'Quran Majid ane Gujarati Tarjumo', *Translation, Mau Abdul Rahim Mav, Gulam Muhamed Sadiq, Sadiq Book Depot, Rander, Surat.*

(4) 'Kuran Sar' *Vinoba Bhave, Yagna Prakashan, Hajur Paga, Vadodara.*

(5) 'Jannat-na-Chalis Rasta', *Shaikhalid Saiyad Ali, Translator Ibrahim Anvar, Darul Ulam Arabiyyah, Bharuch, Mahmudnagar, At P.O. Kantharia, Taluka, Dist. Bharuch.*

(6) 'Jazaul *Aamal Haz. Ma. Ashraf Ali Saheb Thanvi (Rah), Translator Hasan Abdullah Mudkotoovi, Darul Ulam Arabiyyah Islamiyyah, Bharuch, At Post Kanthariya.*

(7) 'Tahid ane Shirkani Hakiquat' *edited by (Mav) Ismail Mohamed Manubari (sa.) Pub. Ulam Arabiyyah Islamiyyah, Bharuch, Mohmoodnagar, At Post: Kanthariya.*

(8) Maaarijun Nabuvvat Sirte Rasule Arabi Sallallaho Alayahe Vasallam, Hazrat Maulana Mulla Muin Vaizal *Kashifo, Pub. Bazme Rukanuddin Nakshabandi Majkedi, Ahmedabad–1.*

(9) 'Shabda ni Katha *Mayamoon', Mayamoon Memorial Publication, Surat.*

(10) 'Sufimat', *Dr. Chhotubhai Ranchhodji Naik, Gujarat Vidyasabha, Amdavad.*